TALES FROM THE BARK SIDE

BY KEITH ALAN ROSS

Best Wishes

TALES FROM THE BARK SIDE

Copyright © 2007 by Keith Alan Ross

Author - Keith Alan Ross
Publisher - McCleery & Sons Publishing

International Standard Book Number: 978-1-931916-52-3

Printed in the United States of America

DEDICATION

*To Lou Hogland and
my lovely wife, Cindy*

ACKNOWLEDGMENTS

*A special thank you to Anna Castillo
and George Kupferschmid for their continuous
support from the very beginning.*

TALES FROM THE BARK SIDE
(THE BOOK)

What started out as an idea in a hallway of a small newspaper office of a relatively small town in rural Minnesota grew into something I previously only dreamed about. That's the magical thing about good ideas... more times than not they come into fruition. Seriously, sometimes it seems when a natural born story teller like me has an idea, it stays that way... just an idea. There has to be something of a grander scale working in order to galvanize those ideas into written form.

It all started with a labor of love... something I have really enjoyed doing since I can remember when; I wrote my wife another poem. That poem was a particularly poignant one (for a humble poet like moi). We used it for our Christmas letter. We decided long ago to put something creative out there for our friends and family instead of a running account of our lives each year. I think it personalizes our letter and gives a little of ourselves in the process. With my wife's flair for the creative, and my penchant for the written word, it has become our yearly communiqué.

I was working in the Perham Enterprise Bulletin building when I happened to engage Lou Hogland (the editor and publisher) in conversation. I didn't work for the paper at the time but I did meet him in the hall quite often. I don't know what prompted me to share that particular poem but I'm glad I did. He compared my work with that of Longfellow and Frost. I was dumbfounded. I thought he was just being kind and way too generous in his praise and assessment... but he still found it to be worthwhile.

Then a kernel of fancy must have struck him. Maybe it was a whimsical moment that caught him in its capricious grip. He asked if I would like to cover a sled dog race in a nearby town for the paper. They do that sort of thing here in Minnesota in the winter. I know it's hard to believe but it is true. I went, I saw, I wrote. Vini Vedi Vechi (that's not really Latin but it looks pretty cool).

Well, back to the hallway where the column found its infancy. The first person color piece was a success and was well received by the man I wanted to impress... Lou Hogland. Having had a modicum of success, I said, "Lou, I have an idea". He smiled and leaned a bit closer. "How about we start a regular column and call it Tales From The Bark Side? He exclaimed, "That's a great idea!"

So, with that said I went home to my lovely wife Cindy and told her the news. She's been a wonderful supporting partner in all other aspects of our lives together and was there from the first day forward cheering me on. She read my copy before I sent it in and with her eye for detail; she has saved me from looking foolish more than once... spel chek suks! As the weeks passed and the tales grew from one paper to another, she was there as my rock, my inspiration, and a great balance to my idiosyncratic ways.

This book is dedicated to Lou and Cindy; Lou for his taking a risk on an unknown writer and Cindy for her unwavering belief in my God given gift. I also want to thank my dearly departed parents, Wilbur and Rosemary Ross, who never had a chance to see my first book published. Still, they both believed in my God given talents. Also, I want to thank the Lord God Almighty. It is He that bestows all our gifts upon us. Thank you Jesus.

Also I want to personally thank all the kind folks who shared their stories of unconditional love for their animals. It's like taking a peek into their souls and I am honored to retell some of these terrific tales. These excursions into the past, where life is played out in Technicolor; where each color on the pallet is a magical moment that endures for years to come, are not about the destination... they are all about the journey.

This book is a collection of stories from my experiences with dogs, cats, and other assorted creatures. Along with my contributions are the tales of the good folk of Ottertail County Minnesota and other regions around the world. You will find 99% of these tales are accurate and totally non-fiction...

the other 1% is editorial license and not intended to lead the reader astray from the real events of that time. I hope you enjoying reading these timeless tales as much I did writing them.

Keith Alan Ross

CHAPTER 1

FROM THE BEGINNING

Ok, first things first. How did I come up with a title that sounds like a rip-off of the HBO series "Tales from the Dark Side"? It is really quite a simple explanation if you think about it. My wife Cindy and I moved from California to Minnesota in the spring of 2002. We bought an eight acre wooded piece of property that allowed me to fulfill one of my dreams... to build a kennel and raise, breed, and train pure bred German Shepherds. We named the property Rosswood and the kennels claimed the same name.

We started with two dogs, then three, then four, and before we knew it, three years later we had eight beautiful dogs of varying ages. Our property is adjacent to a main county road that has lots of summer traffic and being in rural Minnesota very little winter traffic. Pedestrians and cyclists parade past on sunny summer days only to be greeted by a chorus of barking beauties. Throw in the occasional deer trespassing in the night and you have the nocturnal cacophony from within the kennels. This is where the writer in me went amuck. Those who are barked at are the "barkees"; those who bark are the "barkers". We live on the bark side of life here at Rosswood. I have accumulated a treasure trove of timeless tales about dogs and cats and other critters over the years. So when I decided to write the column for the local paper, it only seemed natural to call it, "Tales From The Bark Side". That is the honest truth (not to be confused with the dishonest truth... whatever that is).

When kicking around the idea of actually writing the book version of "Tales", I initially thought I'd do it chronologically. It made sense to me to write about the stories in the order of which they first appeared in my column. Then I thought about it a little more. There is a commonality to almost all of these tales... dogs, cats, raccoons, fowl of all kinds, hamsters, and many other animals which have the ability to reason and problem solve. Where does instinct leave off and intelligence begin? The theme of this book is telling tales about the remarkable things our pets do... and sometimes, their owners.

So with that being said, a tune by Emerson, Lake, and Palmer from the sixties says it all... "From The Beginning".

My folks moved from southern California to the state of Washington in 1948; when I was a year old. Ever since I can remember, there were always cats and dogs in our family. Bootsie (his initial name was Boots) was a cross between a German Shepherd and a Siberian husky... and he resembled a coated (long haired) shepherd in appearance. He was allowed to run freely on our twenty acre farm and he patrolled the front yard like a dedicated sentry.

Bootsie got his name from the four white paws he so prominently displayed. Most of the time they were dirty from his recent exploits and very often as it precipitates in the Evergreen State... muddy. He would lie in wait at the edge of the gravel road that passed in front of our yard. Somewhere off in the distance, on a non rainy day, a fast moving dust cloud would appear and Bootsie would chase after the miscreant auto as it zoomed past the front of our house. He would give up his pursuit after one hundred yards or so and proudly strut back to his waiting position, his tongue hanging out in glorious rapture. He did this all day. He seemed to think that chasing autos was his primary function and a full time job. After all his futile attempts, he never did catch one... but he sure acted as if he did.

This was a behavior that was frowned upon by my dad and mom but nobody seemed to have the time or inclination to modify Bootsie's bad habits. I was a toddler who loved to see the big dog run and I saw no reason to stop him; even if I could.

Bootsie was a fiercely driven dog with tremendous territorial traits that not only pursued passing cars but he kept a keen eye out for four legged invaders too. We had a chicken ranch which at the highest point housed three thousand chickens in three different buildings. Skunks would attempt to prey upon the unsuspecting flock in the middle of the night; seeking out those hens who had laid eggs recently. Bootsie would come to the rescue of the sequestered flock.

One memorable morning, our attention was directed to one of the chicken houses by the loud and vicious barking of our courageous canine. It seemed that Bootsie had cornered a skunk under one of the buildings and was in the process of getting sprayed with skunk juice every time he got close to the black and white fiend. He'd let out with a whelp and then snarl and growl even louder. The smell was stiflingly acrid and nobody in our family would venture out of doors to quell the angered animal.

In retrospect, it seemed like he spent all of the morning repeating this agonizing but courageous act over and over. At some point in this contest of wills, the skunk finally ran out of "perfume" and Bootsie closed in rapidly for the kill. He proudly brought out his prize which he proceeded to shake viciously for at least fifteen minutes. The dead skunk hung like a limp rag and Bootsie dropped it on the ground, then he picked it back up again and shook it some more. He dropped it again and barked at it, perhaps proclaiming in dog language, "Who's the man now?" Looking at the dead skunk being flung about the yard, it was painfully obvious that there wasn't an unbroken bone left in its entire body.

My mom made a tried and true recipe of egg and tomato juice which she applied liberally to Bootsie's coat; which helped knock down the odor somewhat. This formula has been passed down generation to generation and is still a recommended way to deal with skunk odor. The skunk smell seemed to hang around forever, but Bootsie wore his tomato juice suit like a red badge of courage.

As the years passed and eventually, so did the car chasing canine. He was loved dearly but if we knew then what we know now, perhaps he would have been spared an accidental death and lived a longer and more productive life. Looking back in time can teach you important lessons about life, but it can not mend the fractures of an ignorant era.
When Bootsie passed away, we all thought we could never replace such a loyal member of our family; we were wrong. Then came Lady.

Lassie, the famous TV dog, is widely known for her heroics and ability to rescue poor ole "Timmy" from (almost weekly) a number of dangerous situations. How many times can you fall down a well? Of course that was only fiction. Before the long haired fem fatale made her presence known on the silver screen, there was a white collie named Lady who actually did these kinds of things for real. She had the ability to communicate to us that an impending doom was imminent and there was danger present.

Our White Collie, Lady, saved our barn full of summer hay from burning down in the middle of the night. My older brother and I had the illustrious duty of cleaning milking stalls one sultry day during an unusually warm fall in Washington State in the early fifties. The excess straw and accumulated manure was pitched out a window where an electric fence skirted along the side of the rustic structure. A very large pile of the straw and manure mixture was formed next to the thirty year old building and stood there in full sunlight for the rest of the day.

It took many hours of the straw laying across the electric wire to finally ignite and it did sometime after midnight. Lady knew there was something terribly wrong and she was compelled to tell us in her only way. She nearly tore the screen off the back door as she frantically barked and scratched with a tone to her canine voice that meant only one thing; there was immediate danger.

After being abruptly awakened and then peering out the window with half open bleary eyes, my father and older brother raced to the barn which was being consumed with flames. Within minutes of Lady's timely alarm and the aid of lots of water being squirted through two handy hoses, they saved a barn full of summer hay from burning for days.

Lady was rewarded with steak for the next few days. My father was big on rewarding heroes. Lady was a Lassie figure long before Lassie was a household name. She was a remarkable dog in many ways and her exploits may pop up again in this book.

I was impressed at an early age with the intelligence of dogs, and deep inside of me there was germinating a love for them that still exists to this day. It was then and there I knew being involved with canines in some capacity was to be my destiny.

I'm sure many of you may agree with me when I say that dogs are smarter than we ever suspected... they are a lot smarter. They think, they reason, they show love and affection, and gratitude when rescued from dire circumstances. They know when to signal danger when it is necessary. I believe they also have a sense of humor.

Cats on the other hand are sly, cunning, affectionate, but can be aloof much of the time. I believe they are no less intelligent than dogs. I'm not sure cats have a sense of humor but they do know how to get even or, better yet, get their own way. Cats have been known to do heroic feats as well. You might not hear of them sounding the alarm in the middle of the night, or dragging an unconscious person to safety, but they have ways of saving the day... in their own way, of course.

Fritz was a pure bred blue Persian cat who most likely thought he was a dog. The fact that I trained him like a dog might have had something to do with it. Before you avid dog lovers reading this book have a fit, let me explain. Cats can be trained to do certain things, like roll over, beg on their hind legs, and walk an obstacle course like a dog can. Do they have the capacity to communicate alarm or danger? I believe they do. Let me share a tale about a time when Fritz's behavior saved us from a vehicular calamity.

Phoenix in August is unbearably hot for humans to exist in but for a long haired feline, it must have been totally intolerable. I had been living in Scottsdale for about a year and a half and finally made the decision to move back to the bay area. San Jose, California, does get hot in August, but it doesn't even compare to "the Valley of the Sun" (Phoenix) during the dog days of summer. I love the desert and all its botanical glory and the landscape is quite breathe taking in places. I missed the cooler nights and of course, the Pacific Ocean.

Interstate 10 runs through Phoenix and eventually ends up in Los Angeles in the west. It is a freeway that has eight lanes in places and can accommodate a large volume of traffic. It was in the latter part of rush hour traffic on a Friday night when I finally got on the road and with Fritz beside me, in his kennel, we drove into the setting sun at seventy mph. Traffic flowed much faster on the west side of town and a lot of people were headed to Laughlin for gambling or further on to L.A. for the weekend. The highway was crowded that night but traffic zoomed into the west with reckless abandon.

Fritz was a vocal cat that could caterwaul with the best of them. He had a towel draping over his mobile domicile and the air conditioning vent was directed his way; and he had more than enough fresh water. None the less, he started to let me know in no uncertain terms that there was something amiss. Fritz would stick his tongue out at me when he wanted my sole attention. I had learned to recognize this behavior as something out of the ordinary. Can you see this one coming folks?

I'm sure there is a fairly good amount of readers who would agree with the premise that cats have psychic abilities... for that matter, dogs too. I'm not saying that they can read your thoughts but in cases of earthquakes, animals have been observed many times acting strangely before the earth begins to shake, rattle, and roll. There is that sixth sense working in their favor. Some people claim it's a primal need to survive and that they pick up vibrations on a whole different level than we do. I'm not sure what it is, but I've seen the results of this phenomenon first hand.

Fritz continued his yowling with more and more conviction. He was a seasoned passenger in the old 81 Dodge Ram and he traveled in it without any trouble at all... except when there might be danger ahead. I finally pulled off the freeway and found a service station nearby. He caught me in the gaze of those golden amber eyes and let out a staccato "raaant". It was his way to saying thanks for something I had no idea of doing. After a few minutes, I heard the distant cry of police or ambulance sirens approaching from the east. I was in a hurry to get back on the road and continue my sojourn home to California. I returned my feline friend to his kennel and locked it; hoping he had gotten whatever it was out of his system.

I made the turn at the traffic light and entered the on ramp with gusto. I knew how fast they were traveling when I departed I-10 so I was going to match the other vehicles speed with mine. My eyes were awash with a sea of red and all one could see were the flickering red tail lights of what seemed like hundreds of cars.

Traffic had slowed to a crawl and after many laborious minutes of stop and go I found my self being directed into a single lane. The other three lanes were strewn with battered, shattered, and broken automobiles. The early evening was awash with the pulsation of emergency flashers. There was smoke coming from multiple vehicles and people were milling about like refugees of a battle zone.

What caught my eye immediately were two vehicles that I recognized from being side by side with me as we previously had been changing lanes in heavy traffic together. They were twisted like gigantic pretzels and they both emitted plumes of steam and smoke from their demolished motors. But by the grace of God, that would have been Fritz and me among the catastrophic clutter.

I turned off the jazz to which I was listening and dialed in the local news station. After a long while of barely moving and zigzagging through a multiple car pile-up, I picked up speed and continued on my way to California. After listening to the traffic reports from a helicopter overhead, it seems I just missed a fifty car collision with three fatalities.

Fritz hadn't made a sound since we left the gas station. He looked out from his kennel and let go one final "raaant". To this day I truly believe he saved us from mortal danger. Was it coincidence? Was it pure luck on our part? I'll never know for sure, but back in the recesses of my mind I know he saved our lives that night. Thank you, Fritz!

Are dogs and cats psychic? Is there some vibration unheard by humans that only they can perceive? Have you ever observed a pet's behavior change for no apparent reason and minutes later you have relatives or close friends arrive? I'm not suggesting that we have modern day oracles such as Balaam's donkey, but I've seen dogs, cats, cattle, sheep, birds, and many other critters do remarkable things; many times being a harbinger of things to come.

With that said, there are many other beasts residing on the planet who haven't the semblance of a clue; and that includes the human animal as well. The world is wrought with them.

CHAPTER 2

THE COWBOY

Growing up on a farm in rural Washington State was a great place for learning life's lessons at an early age. Some of those lessons still remain succinctly clear in my mind. As adults, we often blame our not so perfect lives on our childhood. For many years I played the "blame game" just like so many other "Baby Boomers". It took me a while, but now I know that we are like stained glass windows... shattered glass can be a beautiful mosaic if you so desire it. Fragments of our past are indelibly etched into our psyches and that is what makes us what we are... a total composite. I had a truly irrational fear of electricity for a very long time. I blamed "Buster" for it. Here's what happened.

My dad had a habit of naming just about everything that walked, crawled, or hopped about on our farm. Each milk cow had her name (Bossey wasn't one of them) and there usually was a story attached to each of them. Pearl was born on December seventh. Her female calf (Harbor) was born on the same day. The fact that my father welded magazine racks on the ships that were sunk in Hawaii in 1941 and left the islands a mere month before the historic attack might have had a little to do with their naming.

Dad usually had a logical reason for naming the critters and Buster was no exception. If my memory serves me correctly, young Buster was a bit of a stall wrecker and he busted out of his confines more than once... hence the name. To say Buster was strong willed would be a gross understatement.

When Buster was a calf, I tried to climb on his back and ride him like a pony or a small horse. He'd just buck me off and run to the other end of the barn yard. I was not to be denied. I tried time and time again, each time finding the landing a bit harder than the attempt before. The beast had to be tamed. I wonder from whom I inherited that stubborn streak. They say the acorn doesn't fall far from the tree. Dad did chase our work horse "Dickey" around the pasture a few times with bridle in hand... not giving up until my mom arrived with sugar cubes and within minutes she had the harried horse under control. I remember her sweet smile as she handed the bridle back to dad.

Being the youngest son of a man who loved his animals (and was stuck in his ways with them) and a woman who spoiled them, I was bound and determined to ride that calf; that was growing faster than me. A brilliant thought came to me one day. Okay, it wasn't so brilliant but it seemed like the right thing to do at the time. That's the way most ideas start.

We had a section of the barn where the cattle could

come in from the weather and find comfort and solace in the protection of the rickety old barn. One day I decided to wait there for Buster to come in with the rest of our small herd, and from my perch next to the opening, I would leap upon his back and away we would go.

Evidently, Buster had other ideas on the subject of being ridden. He bellowed some unmistakable signal to the rest of his bovine family and they came running out of the barn in what one could call a miniature stampede. I was atop of Buster trying valiantly to find a way to hang on. White faced Herefords don't have a mane like a horse. He didn't even have horns big enough on which to hang.

I can't remember just how far I made it before being flung into the plentiful and awaiting barnyard dung. I was literally a shitty mess but was beaming like a winner of the Kentucky Derby. I was convinced that it would be just a matter of time before I would be astride Buster for the entire world to see. Me, a real "cow" boy.

The amazing thing about it all was the fact that Buster was becoming more accepting with each passing day, of having a rider upon his back. First, it was a minute or two that I stayed on his back. Then it was up to five long minutes and then up to ten; and so on. I was wearing the bovine beast down with each successful attempt. Maybe it was at this point

in my life that I got on track with training animals...
or not! I couldn't see or hear the metaphorical freight
train headed my way.

I became so full of confidence with my abilities to
"break" Buster and ride him almost like a horse that
I took to bringing along a comic book; which I read
while being on top of the hefty Hereford. He had
been growing at a rapid rate but I wasn't. I was
becoming a legend in my own mind as I sat atop of
him like a proud cowhand coming back from a month
long cattle drive along the Chisom Trail.

Some of life's lessons are learned by paying
attention in class. Some are taught by hands on
instruction by an experienced person. Other lessons
are the direct result of personal involvement in
something that has the most negative impact without
the most negative results. I call these lessons of
mistaken assumptions.

It was another warm and sunny summer day and I
had ridden (loose interpretation here) Buster to the
far edge of our twenty acres. To a child of six, it was
an enormous amount of property. He was grazing
away with no thought towards where he was headed
(other words, clueless). An electric fence skirted
along side a neighbor's field, and the grass always
being greener on the other side of the fence, stood
between Buster and a large tuft of tasty turf.

I was oblivious. I had a "Superman" comic book out and the man of steel was being faster than a speeding bullet. My enthrallment was not long lasting. The Hereford stretched his neck as far as was physically possible and that wasn't quite far enough to munch that last clump of grass that sat there so invitingly. He gave another lunge and the wire that hung there so innocuously came in contact with the top of his shoulders... inches away from where I was lounging in luxury.

The bellow that caused the other cattle to bolt from the barn months before was but a whisper in comparison to the wild cry that issued forth from Buster's frantic lungs. The young bull bellowed again in writhing pain. We were being electrocuted. I felt the pain coarse through my body like a tidal wave. I found out that large animals (at that age, anything bigger than a dog was a large animal) conduct electricity extremely well.

My self righteous world was shocked back into reality. I can't begin to tell you how much that shot of voltage scared me that day. It also scarred me too. Buster never let me come near him again. I quit trying to master him and couldn't get back up on that metaphorical horse (in this case a bull) that threw me. Some days later I was flying a kite and fell backwards into another section of that very same electric fence. It re-enforced my fear of electricity to the point that I avoided it at all costs.

I learned humility at an early age. I thought it was so cool riding on the back of Buster. Buster stayed pretty much in the middle of the field for a long time thereafter. We both learned. Now I can change light fixtures without any trepidation but back when I was a child of six, I had the shock of my life. What happens to us when we are young also helps mold us into what we are going to be in the future.

I had a lot of barnyard adventures when I was but a young lad, but not all these tales of misadventures on a farm belong only to me. In my column, I have received more than several tales concerning high drama in and around the fragrant yard of a barn.

My wife was raised in rural Minnesota five years after I was born and her life on a farm was not unlike mine. She also had an older brother who was an instigator of more than one nefarious (the dictionary claims the word to be flagrantly wicked) excursion around their parent's and grandparent's farms. Maybe nefarious isn't quite the right word but he seemed to get her in trouble like older brothers have a propensity to do.

My lovely wife Cindy delved back into her memory banks to recall a time on her grandparent's farm. It was in the fifties and she was five years old and her brother Michael was seven. As children will do sometimes, they were bent on mischief (actually the older brother was the ring leader and my lovely wife was the poor misled sister) and it was found by teasing a barnyard rooster into chasing them; well, actually it only chased Michael. Michael claims he had the get away planned perfectly, but it was the gate keeper's fault that his well engineered plot went astray.

Cindy's job was to be the tender of the gate and to open it, letting her brother in when the rooster chased him to the front yard of their grandparent's house. When the brother arrived with the angry rooster hot on his tail, Cindy couldn't get the gate to unlatch fast enough and have it open for her forlorn and screaming brother's arrival. This set her off and both of them jumped up and down and started crying in unison... two part hysterical harmony.

The grandparents and parents were in the house doing what adults do, visiting. Then, all of a sudden they heard the two children wailing away like they have just had a catastrophic accident and were both at death's door. They came running with which any caring parent can relate; abject fear for their children's safety and well being. Upon realizing that their offspring were being terrorized by a strutting cock of a rooster, they broke out in near riotous mirth. Their sides ached with relief and they were glad that they weren't hurt or injured.

This ebullience from the elders came to the dismay of the crying children who, after Cindy got the gate finally open, stopped sobbing long enough to see the rooster strutting away in a huff. Evidently, he thought it better to leave screaming kids alone.

So much for the best laid plans of older brother and little sister. They also learned an important lesson that day, and it wasn't "leave sleeping dogs lie" either. What can seem tragic at the time, can turn on the head of a pin and be a wonderful learning experience. The years of innocence play out on Bill Shakespeare's stage only to be reviewed by harsh critics later on in life.

Hind sight seemingly is twenty twenty and we can see our past transgressions ever so clearly from the comfort of our reclining years; but that's what tales are for. They can shine a uniquely different light upon that which was once dark or revisit that which was humorous with new found affection. It's all in the telling.

CHAPTER 3

BANDIT AND TWEETY

I think it's rather curious how you may start one thing and end up doing another. My editor, Lou Hogland, at the Perham Enterprise Bulletin wrote a little article about two of our younger female shepherds here at Rosswood Kennels. It wasn't that it was poorly written, which it surely wasn't. It was not entirely factual. He had the names of the dogs reversed and added that I waded in the pond with hip waders (which I don't even own). I don't blame Lou one iota because I have done the same thing myself... getting the facts askew with antidotal information.

As I mentioned before, I shared a poem with him and he gave me an assignment that catapulted my writing into something all together different than poetry. I embraced the column with inexperienced vigor and zeal but held true to keeping the facts straight. I found that it was really hard to re-tell a tale without bruising the flesh of a very ripe intellectual fruit. It was all about the story. I found out that it didn't have to be absolutely correct, because it was a story... and I am a story teller.

If it was a news item that I was working on that needed clear and unbiased reporting (like that ever happens), I wouldn't have the same attitude toward the content of the tales that I tell. I get as close to the "truth" as one can get without being too anal about the details and thus make an interesting story boring and unimaginative. When these letters come across my desk, I try to glean as much information as I can from them without losing the sparkle of the tale.

Do you know the exercise about the circle and how the tale being told changes from one person to another? When the story finally reaches the original teller, it has become something altogether different. It's kind of like that when I'm jotting down notes from an excited person who has those wonderful memories to share with me. I try to stay focused on the story itself without embellishing it too much. With that said, I will share these gems from my readers as we go along.

Last chapter I told a tale my wife shared with me. When it was published, I didn't have all the facts of the story straight, but the version I recount in Chapter Two is as close to the actual truth as it can be. The very first tale from somebody other than myself or my wife was from Glen Lutz. I was guilty of not having all the facts straight but I found out later that both Glen and his wife Barbara had different versions of the same tale. See what I mean? The article ran in the local weekly paper and it went something like this.

If you have been to the Otter Supper Club, in Ottertail, a couple of years ago, you would have found our contributor working over in the off sale area. He's none other than the personable Glen Lutz. Glen had a pet raccoon that rode in the back seat of his car, picked ice from the drinks of patrons in drinking establishments, and swatted curious coon hounds that got too close for comfort. But this story isn't about those shenanigans; it's about a yellow canary.

Glen had a yellow canary that he kept in a cage in the living room. He had the bird about a week and hadn't gotten around to naming it yet. I will take editorial license and call him "Tweety" because it just sounds better than "the bird". The raccoon's name was "Bandit" and he was sent outside like a cat or dog when "Tweety" was let out of his cage to exercise. Some days Glen would come home and Tweety would be outside of his cage and flying about the inside of the house and Bandit would be sitting there licking his chops waiting for the most auspicious moment to make his move.

Of course, Glen's two sons would get the blame for not putting Bandit outside before letting the bird (Tweety) out of his domicile when the curious coon was at large on the premises. The sons pleaded their innocence and had told their dad that they had no idea how Bandit got back in the house. All the doors and windows were shut tight. Because of the boys' prior transgressions and liberties with the truth, Glen chose to think they were not owning up to their alleged irresponsible behavior.

On the day of Tweety's demise, all was found out how Bandit was managing to be in the house at the same time poor ole Tweety was out of his cage. Glen came home to feathers on the floor of the kitchen and a raccoon in the living room looking like the proverbial cat that ate you know what... the canary! Bandit was banished from the house at once. A few minutes passed and strange noises from the back porch could be heard. Glen quietly snuck back through the kitchen and peeked around the door to the porch and beheld quite a site. A miniature furry hand was reaching through an empty pane of glass in the storm door, flipping up the lever handle, and successfully opening the door. The mystery was solved and the sons were exonerated from their father's false accusations. I have a question or two though.

First of all, a raccoon is still a wild animal and has all its natural instincts intact, right? With all the birds and rodents and whatever outside the house to prey upon, why did the raccoon choose to break and enter to commit the crime of killing the canary? Did he just domesticate to the point where he wanted to be around people and in a jealous rage killed his yellow feathered rival? Was it a crime of passion or was it premeditated to occur when nobody was in the house? We'll never know.

Glen still chuckles to himself when recalling those raccoon adventures. I would too. I'm forever being amazed at the native intelligence domestic animals and creatures of the wild possess. You can raise almost any animal to be a pet but not every animal. Be very careful in choosing your pet so that it fits in with your lifestyle, your family needs, and your ability to care for it. By domesticating any animal you must bear the responsibility for that creature's health and welfare.

While we're on the subject of raccoons, I might as well mention an event that occurred here at Rosswood shortly after we arrived from sunny California. Continuing the tradition that my father so generously did with all walks of life, I named our eight acres "Rosswood". They are heavily wooded acres and all sorts of nocturnal beasties go scampering through them at all hours of the night.

This particular occasion happened before we took possession of a small pack of German Shepherds. It was a time before our dogs alerted on the movements of deer and other assorted wild life. In other words, it was mortuary quiet... very quiet so that you could hear almost everything that transpired outside our window to the world. This is a tale from the un-barked side of life.

My wife is a rather sound sleeper and in my natural state, I am not; blame it on Viet Nam or just an active mind that doesn't shut off easily. Since I had recently under gone back surgery, the pain meds and muscles relaxants I took assured me of at least six solid hours of deep sleep. Cindy and I were getting used to the house, its nocturnal noises and the lack thereof. Coming from the San Francisco bay area (and all the tumult, chaos, and city traffic noises) we weren't quite used to it being so dog gone quiet (no pun intended).

Cindy woke up first. I was still groggy enough to not quite comprehend the source of her agitation... she was sitting straight up in bed and shaking me with the vigor only a loving and trusting wife can muster. I was her knight. She was semi scared and semi curious... I was semi conscious.

Down below our second story bedroom window we heard a scraping or dragging noise. At first I thought it might be rain in the gutter making that awful sound that can keep you awake for hours. I was urged to get out of bed and find out what the commotion was all about. I shrugged myself into my robe, tied the belt with a flourish, and reached for my weapon.

I had purchased a three million candle power industrial strength flash light that would give most people a "close encounter of a third kind" experience... we're talking beams shot down from a mother ship bright! I had my trusty flashlight and I figured if worse came to worst, I could blind an intruder or even hit them over the head with it. It had a fair amount of weight to it. I was armed but maybe not so dangerous. Remember the back surgery?

I made my way down the stairs and crossed the living room like Inspector Clouseau (the Pink Panther) tracking my prey with the stealth of a Sherman Tank. The light was flashing off windows, nearly blinding me twice, and the first floor of our once peaceful house was flooded with an ethereal white light. Cindy waited at the head of the stairs cheering her gallant husband forward into the unknown.

I stepped out into the cool of the summer evening and slowly rotated the beam of light around the yard. I'd almost swear that ships at sea on both coasts could see our beacon shining away; well, maybe not both coasts. I pointed it in every direction imaginable. I surveyed trees with the light, and covered the surrounding grounds with great care and anticipation... nothing!

I was such a dismal failure at finding the intruder but I held true to the thought that in my clumsy and meager attempt to find out what was going on, I had inadvertently chased the burglar away. That was my story and I was sticking to it.

I returned to bed and after a conversation with the wife about how I scared the bad guys away, we both found our way back to slumber and the night wore on until daybreak. At breakfast I went outside to take the trash out and found the large Steve's Sanitation two wheel trash can pulled away from the wall of the garage. The lid was open and the contents were still inside but it was somewhat of a mystery as to what or who had pulled the half full trash can so far from the house. We both thought it could have been a coon.

It wasn't until later in the day that the mystery was solved... at least to Cindy's and my satisfaction. Out on the road was the largest raccoon I have ever seen in my life; lying dead along County Highway 1. He was obviously hit by a passing motorist sometime in the wee hours of the morning. If I were to guess, he must have weighed at least 45 to 55 pounds.

In my mind's eye, I could see him pushing on the container and it rolling away from him... the bottom scraping the driveway. He managed to flip the lid but I believe every time he tried to climb inside, the trash can rolled backwards again. I know raccoons are not fond of bright light and he must have high tailed it out of Dodge before the human strobe light arrived on the scene.

They are really smart and agile creatures but what bothers me is how they get killed by automobiles so often. It must be the car's high beams that freeze them in the middle of the road. The next year found us with an abundance of barking canines and the raccoons have not bothered us again. Rosswood was becoming the "bark side of life" but there was a time when we were without the early warning system we both now cherish.

Before we leave the subject of raccoons, I have another short tale to tell. A very nice woman who lives about two miles from Rosswood submitted this tale to me. Bobbi Goetz Nelson lives right on Ottertail Lake and has her share of adventures to recount, but this particular one illustrates how nocturnal creatures can be dissuaded from your premises with an invention from Tommy Edison; not totally unlike my luminescent adventure. Here's Bobbi's tale.

Here is my raccoon story. One evening a few years ago, I was sitting in my big chair, reading a book, when out of the corner of my eye, I saw an animal run across the room. At first, I thought it was my little dog "Cannolli", but realized that she was sitting next to me. Then for a second, I thought it was the neighbor's cat, but when I saw the striped tail, I knew it was a raccoon. Apparently, it came into the house through the dog door.

The raccoon ran to a lower room on the entrance level (chased by my barking dog) and hid behind a couch. I tried for a long time, without success, to get the raccoon outside by poking him with a long stick. He in turn fought the stick with his long claws.

At this point I decided to barricade this lower level so that my dog and I would be safe upstairs, and think this problem out a bit. I went back to my book and read a chapter to give the three of us (raccoon, doggie, and me) a rest. Then I remembered that raccoons don't like the light so I turned the lights on bright in the raccoon's room. I opened the outside door and turned the lights out in the entrance hall. I poked the raccoon again with my long stick and out he went into the night and I returned to my book.

Thank you, Bobbi, for your contribution. As Sonny and Cher once put it so eloquently, "The Beat Goes On". And so shall we.

CHAPTER 4

HELLO DAWG

When you take a journey back in time to where people and places are but a blur to your memory, only the truly distinct events stand out in your mind. There are so many things that happen to a young person growing up in this world, that those kinds of things get lost in the daily mental shuffle we use to deal with life.

My life and times as a child helped pave a road I would travel for the rest of my life. In Viet Nam, it would be "Thunder" road. Looks like I'm getting ahead of myself again, so I should tell a tale about my early army years that you might find interesting. Almost 99.9 % of this tale is true and accurate. I have embellished and altered only a few little things in it to protect the innocent (that being me). All in all, these things did happen and disclaimer aside, it left a distinct impression upon me even to this day.

In 1966, I joined the U.S. Army. I did my basic training at Fort Ord on the Monterey Peninsula during the month of March. We had a wonderful view of the bay when we were crawling on our bellies through what seemed like miles of sand. The rifle range was on a beach overlooking miles of unfettered dunes. I have always loved going to the beach but not carrying a pack that weighed over seventy five pounds.

I had two weeks leave in May and I was headed to the Deep South. Fort Gordon was near Augusta, Georgia (which we called Disgusta) and was basically located in a swamp. I went through Military Police School thinking I had just about enough training to last me a lifetime. The summers in Georgia aren't a whole lot of fun either; and being harassed by some idiot drill sergeant wasn't too thrilling to say the least. We collectively hated the place. It was the Army's way of creating unity amongst the troops.

The day came when we all awaited our next duty assignment with great anticipation. Anything would be better than where we were...well almost anything. There still was Nam awaiting us across the Pacific Ocean. Of course, I conveniently forgot that there were even hotter places to be assigned to in the states and just hoped and prayed that I would go to Europe. Almost all my Military Police Company did go to Germany... but not me. I got to go to another school for more training... whoopee!!!

The flight to San Antonio Texas was on a DC3...I'm not kidding... it was so old that we wondered which one was flying... Orville or Wilbur. West Texas in August and September is unbearable... temps in the low one hundreds are normal. We landed and were transported to an air base; Lackland Air Force Base to be exact.

We thought we went to heaven. Our room accommodated four men which beat the painful reality of fifty men snoring together in discordant harmony. The Air Force does their basic training there, so when we walked by formations of raw recruits with no stripes on our sleeves and brass on our collars, it was delightful to have them call the formation to attention and salute us... just for us lowly privates. I was beginning to like the place.

Why was I on an Air Force base when I was in the Army? Good question. Lackland was the only military installation that had a Sentry Dog School. I was going to be a dog handler. But first we had to have two weeks of book learning. They just didn't give you a dog and let you have at it. You had to know about parasites, grooming techniques, and the general philosophy of dog training. The dogs had to be treated with respect and taught to obey from a place of loyalty to their master.

During this time of classroom training, rumors flew about like wind blown butterflies. There was one particular rumor we all had an interest in... who would get Sully? Sully was a legendary German Shepherd that was very large, aggressive, and very smart. The several soldiers that had tried to handle Sully were bitten severe enough to be medically discharged from the service. It seems that when Sully couldn't stand the West Texas heat, he'd bite his handler and would be taken back to his much cooler kennel. Smart dog... and dangerous too.

We dreaded each day with forlorn fear. "Please God, don't let it be me" each man silently prayed. As the days grew closer to when we would go to the kennels and meet our dogs, it seems a pool was started by the Non Commissioned Officers that ran the place. The odds weren't too good for anyone. It was thought that whoever was unlucky enough to draw Sully wasn't going to make it through the day without being bitten severely. We all knew that deep down in the fiber of our souls.

Finally the fateful day arrived like a black sunrise. The air was still and the thermometer was climbing steadily towards one hundred degrees again. No one uttered a word. Breakfast was eaten in silence...each man alone in his thoughts. Then the march to the kennels in formation... nobody called cadence that day. It was the darkest hour and the snickers from the trainers was deafening. Like lambs to the slaughter we marched... choke chains jingling in the morning sun.

We arrived at the kennels to be greeted by a cacophony of barking dogs... some growling and some snarling, but some dogs just were driven by anxiety; much like their would be masters. One by one the soldiers names were called and then the name of their canine comrade. All waited to hear Sully's name to be read.

John Stevens (fictitious name to protect the guilty party) was from the hills of Tennessee... a true hillbilly if there ever was one. He stood six foot four inches barefooted; which I think had been his normal state of attire most of his life. John had flaming orange red hair that was cut in a flat top. Freckles were scattered across his face like the shot pattern of a twelve gauge shotgun on a paper target.

When he heard his name called, John smiled that lackadaisical smile of his and said, "Thank ya suh." An E.F. Hutton hush fell upon the gathered throng. We watched him turn on his heels and march promptly towards his destiny... all one hundred man eating pounds of him. What happened next was extraordinary.

John reached Sully's kennel and just stood there staring at the animal. The non commissioned officers held their collective breaths. Sully was tethered on a kennel chain that measured ten feet. As long as you stayed the appropriate distance from him, you were relatively safe. The snarling dog crept closer and closer hoping his next victim would step inside the ten foot radius. John just stood there... in deep concentration it seemed... or in mortal fear. The crowd of onlookers kept their distance but they craned their necks to hear anything... even a whisper.

All at once John lunged forward with such speed it shocked his captive audience. His right arm was raised above his head with his right hand balled into a fist. He struck Sully right between the ears with such ferocity that the dog's legs buckled and he felled upon his front feet like a bow a performer gives at the end of a performance; his lower jaw horizontal with the ground.

"HELLO DAWG", John half yelled and screamed. He reached in and grabbed the surprised shepherd by the collar and yanked him to his feet. "HOW YA DOIN' DAWG? He drawled again at the top of his lungs. The defeated dog fell to John's feet. John reached down and placed a choke chain around Sully's neck and removed that leather collar in one deft motion that would draw envy from a Vegas blackjack dealer.

"LET'S GO DAWG", he commanded the bewildered beast. The two of them headed out of the kennels to the practice field where John put Sully through his paces. The onlookers were completely astonished and revolted at John's technique but soon come to understand the dynamics involved. Sully had never met an Alpha male before. The hillbilly from Tennessee was definitely in charge and the miscreant dog soon learned that he wasn't in charge any more.

I remember the training staff yelling at Stevens that he was going to get himself killed doing that to a very dangerous dog. John replied, "He ain't so dangerous, mean dogs are like skinning a mule, you gotta hit em up side the head to get their attention, then ya lets em know who's boss."

The dog never tried to bite him. I don't recommend that training technique, but on that day in the sweltering heat of West Texas, a country boy knew better than the pros. To this day, I can still hear him out on the practice field with the infamous killer dog yelling, "HELLO DAWG, GOOD DAWG, SIT DAWG, STAY DAWG and my favorite, "SICKEM DAWG!!!"

The two were meant for each other. I'll never forget the expressions on the Non Commissioned Officer's faces. Please forgive the pun, but in the Army, there was always more than one way to skin a cat; or train a dog. Suffice it to say, I picked an interesting career path and that path (or road) twisted and turned through many a clime and scape. Tales are often told along the side of the road of life... some of them at the end and some of them are reflections along the way. I believe it's the journey that makes the measure of a man (and woman as well). Shall we journey forth together?

CHAPTER 5

A BOMBS AND WILD CATS

Being a sentry dog handler in the Army meant one or two things... most Non Commissioned Officers didn't exactly know what you were supposed to do on a daily basis; the Commissioned Officers didn't entirely trust the process of having a dog be the main defense against infiltrators. Consequently, there was always some degree of mystery to what we did... many times to our own chagrin.

My first tour of duty stateside was to walk around a Nike Hercules Missile battery that overlooked the San Fernando Valley. When I left Lackland Air Force base with a smallish German Shepherd named Dude, I was more than glad to be out of there and be rid of a nickname I picked up. Because Dude only weighed fifty five pounds I had the moniker "Fox Handler" bestowed upon me by none other than the hillbilly himself... John Stevens. I took a daily razzing from him that could only be resolved by our parting and following our own path towards destiny.

The thought of being near Los Angeles was very appealing to me for many reasons... the girls were gorgeous and I was nineteen. Enough said about that! I flew into LAX in a conventional air liner and Dude was safely tucked away underneath the belly of the huge aircraft. Eventually, I was greeted by two men in uniform (they actually were in the Army) who had an olive drab colored Ford Econoline. Since that ride up into the San Gabriel Mountains, I have shied away from riding in anything that has the word "Econo" on it.

The military used to transport canines in these large aluminum crates that were bulky and when left out in the sun, became very warm to the touch... maybe hot is a better word. We were transported (dumped) on the tarmac adjacent to the cargo area in the blazing southern California sun... and we waited and we waited. Dude couldn't get out of the kennel because the concrete was too hot for him to walk upon; so I sat hunched down next to him for what seemed like an eternity.

Finally Homer and Jethro (fictious names) arrived with the aforementioned van that seemed to lean to one side. Apparently shocks weren't on the maintenance list that week. I climbed into the back of the van and tried to hang on to anything I could find. The ride down the freeway was bad enough but when we got to the mountain curves of the Sand Canyon Road, it became brutal. I think Homer (maybe it was Jethro) wanted see if he could make me carsick with the way he was negotiating the turns... remember the shocks? I had a vision of us tumbling down the canyon side. Dude was attempting to give me dirty looks from within the crate and I knew he was not pleased with his master at that particular time.

We arrived and were greeted by the commanding officer and then shown to my quarters and also where to take Dude. They had three other sentry dogs assigned there and I was number four. Oh, did I mention that the tips of these Nike Hercules Missiles were adorned with a thermal nuclear warhead? I found out that little fact after fifteen minutes on base. Suddenly, my love affair with my California assignment grew most assuredly colder. Anti war protesters hadn't twitched to that fact either... Thank God!

It wasn't high stress pins and needles kind of work; walking a dog around a double fence line in the middle of the night. In fact, for a high strung nineteen year old male, it was pretty boring. Nobody was charging up the hill trying to over run our facility. The days turned into months and the routine was probably our worst enemy.

The gentlemen (I'm using this term loosely) who were the Officers of the Day would periodically try to catch us dog handlers unawares or maybe just goofing off when we should have been tending to business as usual. They would walk, instead of ride up the paved road leading to the missile silos. These great thinkers had the notion that they could "sneak" up on us. A dog's nose is forty times more effective than a human's and even with a minimal breeze, a dog can smell a person hundreds of yards away.

After halting and placing an officer in the prone (face down) position on the pavement one night, it seemed I must have passed some sort of test. My commanding officer told me I could trust the duty officers to be who they are and not to search them in the manner in which I did. I said yes sir with the straightest face I could muster and planned to do exactly what I had done before. It was a top secret facility and being a buck private, I was at the bottom of the military food chain. I planned to cover my assets by being alert and on top of things every night I walked the dog. This was easier said than done.

It was this frame of mind that I brought with me the night Dude and I encountered a wild beast caught inside the double fence. I went to high school in the "Silicon Valley" (Actually it's the Santa Clara Valley) and a small town nestled in the foothills of that valley was Los Gatos. In Spanish, it means 'The Cats' and was named for the wildcats that prowled the hills at night. We're not talking about feral cats that have gone wild from their domestic domiciles. The California Bobcat (Lynx Rufus) is a ferocious feline that preys upon just about anything it wants.

I had the third watch that night... 3 A.M. to 6 A.M. or sunrise (whichever came first). Dude wasn't the most aggressive graduate coming out of sentry dog school. He had one thing that every dog handler in all of the armed services coveted; he had a world class nose.

He was a pretty boy that although he was slight in stature, he was tremendously quick and strong. He'd pull your arm off if you let him. My saving grace in all this was that I had trained him and he was dedicated and obedient to me.

In the dark, a human being can't make out distinct details of objects that they might encounter... but a canine partner surely can. They see objects in the dark ten times further away than their masters. So, when we came upon this dark shape in the interior fence line, Dude already knew what we were up against. I wouldn't say I didn't have a clue but my vision was limited to only so far away. Dude began to pull on his leash with the strength Ben Hur's chariot horses would admire.

He barked that alarm bark. Maybe a lot of people have experienced that themselves; when their dogs detected danger and alerted the family to a forth coming intruder. Dude saw an intruder and snarled his way forward with me hanging on for dear life... my boot heels digging into the pea gravel with no or very little affect.

Finally the Bobcat found the hole in the fence from

whence it came and then clamored back down the mountain to a shoulder that jutted out just below the kennels. Dude tried his best to go under the fence that had been dug out by the intruding feline but I held on the best I could. It just so happened that there was an entry gate that went from the corner of the fence line down to the kennels. It was built so that the dog handlers wouldn't have to walk all the way around to the front of the main gate area. I opened it up and we both continued to pursue the miscreant cat farther down the hill... and away from my assigned post. We were in hot pursuit. By this time I had my .45 out and was wondering to myself how I was going to explain shooting a Bobcat fifty yards away from my post.

Sometimes when the proverbial is hitting the fan, you have a moment of clarity. I couldn't let the cat come and go as it pleased and put my dog and myself at risk. I couldn't really shoot it without getting myself in a heap of trouble. What to do? I wrapped Dude's leash around my left arm and reached down and picked up a good sized rock with a fair amount of heft to it and wound up and hit it at the shoulders with a fastball swing of my right arm. It let out a screech and bolted over the fence in a low area below the kennels. I felt bad about hurting it but I'm convinced it wouldn't have felt bad about hurting both Dude and me.

Whoever said, "Discretion is the Better Part of

Valor" was absolutely correct; especially on that dark and dreadful night in the San Gabriel Mountains above L.A. After eight months of stateside duty, I volunteered for Viet Nam... so much for discretion. Like a hideously black thunder cloud that loomed in the distance, the little country that was once called Siam, waited for me.

CHAPTER 6

OF GENERALS AND BOSUN MATES

Many times our pets are like family to us and even those folks who have to move around a lot in their service to their country would agree... it feels like home when you have your pet friend by your side. Other than my working dogs, I wasn't in the service long enough to have base housing where I could have my own pet. Those that were higher up in rank, in all services, found it necessary to have a faithful pet along for the journey. This tale which I like to tell is about a dog that didn't walk a perimeter like Dude or the aforementioned Thunder... he sprinted!

Helen Burns of Perham, Minnesota sent me a tale about the time she and her husband, Eddie (who were enlisted in the Air Force together) had the privilege to share their quarters with a General. Here's their story.

It all started at a pound near Barksdale Air Force Base, Louisiana in 1963. They came upon this one and a half pound black puppy that looked like a dachshund mix. He was being stepped on and mistreated badly by his other companions in the pound. The owner of the establishment said he had no place for the pup and he felt it would not live long. They took him to a Vet and were told the same thing "Won't live through the night". The courageous canine had a different opinion; as they often do.

Not only did he manage to survive but he grew into seven pounds of holy terror and into being the ranking canine on the base. General Doodles was his name and he acted like he was in charge. He carried his food dish every where he went and guarded it jealously... he didn't like kids and most adults. He was a real charmer.

He would race the entire length of the fenced in yard chasing the KC-135 jets that were being scrambled into the clear blue cloudless sky. He would stand in "his" yard, with his head pointed towards the horizon and growl his celebratory growl for having chased the noisy jets away.

The General was relentless in his quest to get outside his domain; harnesses and gates and fences did little to dissuade him. The opinion was that he was a big dog in a little dog's body. A hook was put on his harness one time and Eddie and Helen returned home to find him hanging on the gate with a guilty look on his face. He was held captive by his own designs and he had places to go and people to bark at.

Seven years passed and the Burns's transferred to Little Rock AFB and their daughter found a small and stinky dachshund that was very unlike the General... it was cute and cuddly. A show down was imminent. Doodles didn't want to share his yard but since Puddles was scared of every living (and some not living) thing, they soon became buddies. It was part of the GDPP (General Doodles Protection Plan).

As time went on, the couple got another dog... this time a Bassett Hound named Arki. Duty stations changed but the triad of hounds had their way of making life interesting. Arki chased toads and sat on the General from time to time; nearly smothering him to death in his declining years. The General lasted sixteen years and lived life on his terms. Eddie and Helen are retired from the service, but memories of their times together with their canine companions will continue even beyond their years.

The expression, "It's not the size of the dog in the fight, it's the size of the fight in the dog" bears remembering. Although he was a physical threat and nuisance to friends and neighbors, he lived his life on his terms and his size wasn't the determining factor of how he did it. Thanks Eddie and Helen Burns for your heartwarming tale.

Growing up, we all have heard the phrase, "Dynamite comes in a small package". The General definitely filled the bill on that sentiment but when that small package comes in the form of a ferocious feline, all canines better beware.

Howard Seiple of New York Mills once had a cat that was the terror of an entire Naval Base. I'm sure he was smiling when he wrote his tale about the "Bosun's Mate". Here it is in Howard's own words.

This is a fun story about the BOSUN (A Navy short name for a boatswain mate) who happened to be a base mascot cat.

I was going to parachute school at Naval Air Station (N.A.S.) Lakehurst, N.J. as a part of my naval training in 1949. At our mess hall was a large old cat, which had been through some battles, that we called the BOSUN. He only had half a tail and part of an ear was gone but he was our mascot and he was friendly to all; well, all people that is.

One day a LIEUTENTANT (JG) came on the base with a Dalmatian. The base C.O. told him to get rid of the dog but before he did, the LT. brought the dog with him to the officer's mess hall (which was across from ours). Well, the dog saw the BOSUN and went in for the kill. Biggest mistake that dog made in his life. In about one minute BOSUN almost took that dog apart.

The dog took off for parts unknown and didn't come back until the next day. Ole BOSUN went back to his bed by the mess hall and went to sleep. One angry and visibly upset JG went to the base commander and demanded that the cat be removed from the base immediately. The commanding officer politely reminded the junior officer that "Bosun" was the "base mascot" and that dogs weren't allowed on base in the first place. The LT. didn't bring his dog with him again! They say that rank has its privileges and on that day, a straggly looking feline outranked a Dalmatian by a few stripes (and swats).

Not all dogs and cats behave as arch enemies and I believe that has a lot to do with how they were raised as pups and kittens. Environment plays an important part in the development of an animal's personality. When raised as puppies and kittens together, they often form a bond stronger than that of a representative of the same specie. We (as humans) instill a certain amount of animus between the two by creating a rivalry that sometimes isn't too healthy. "They fought like cats and dogs" is a phrase that illustrates a predisposition on the matter. Most animals will get along well when left to their own devices. I can't say the same for us humans, though.

CHAPTER 7

MR. SQUIRRELLY

As I previously have said, this isn't an autobiographical book but one that is a compilation of stories that come from my adventures with animals of all sorts and those of my readers of the newspaper column "Tales From The Bark Side". These wonderful people have shared their memories, their heartaches from the loss of a treasured friend, and the general misadventures that their four legged (and sometimes the two legged) companions get themselves into.

This journey that I have taken in writing "Tales From The Bark Side" has had a few curves in it and many times it's been a pleasant surprise to find these little nuggets along the way. My readers vary in age, but quite a few of them qualify as seasoned citizens. They all have that one thing in common; they have all unconditionally loved their pets with every fiber of their tender hearts.

As I began to write my column for the Perham Enterprise Bulletin and the weekly shopper known as the Contact, it became clear to me that there was this vast store house of stories just waiting to be opened. I think it must be like that for many a person who starts something without an end goal in mind. You just go where the stories lead you and along the way you are exposed and treated to some of the most charming tales... and being a story teller, I was hooked.

Rosswood Kennels is aptly named and you can't have a stand of trees in Minnesota without the obligatory number of squirrels skittering across your yard at all hours of the day. I've had my battles with the furry creatures and they still plague us to this day but they are respectful of our shepherds and keep their distance accordingly.

A man who also writes a column for a nearby town wrote to me describing an encounter with a bushy tailed rodent he called "Mr. Squirrelly". Ike Fischer lives in Frazee, Minnesota and writes for the Frazee Forum. Thank you once again, Ike, for your recollections of a past adorned with great adventures. Here is Ike's tale.

In the mid-thirties when I was about 12 years old, we found a baby grey squirrel that must have lost its mother and was starving, and too weak to run away from us. It was mostly head and tail with a skinny body in between.

Having lots of fresh, warm milk on the farm back then, we held some to his mouth with a spoon and shortly he began to lap at the milk like a cat.

We brought him into the house and tucked him into the pocket of a large overcoat my uncle used to wear in the coldest weather. The coat was hanging on the bedroom door where it was warm and the squirrel felt secure and he stayed there until we took him out to feed him milk again.

We would put him outside during the day but nights he would retire to its coat pocket. When it was outside with us, he stayed close but sometimes we'd have to leave him but "Squirrelly" knew where the door was and he waited on the porch roof above the door. He would wait until someone came to go in, then would jump on their shoulder and ride into the house with them.

He easily became "house broken" and as he grew we fed him peanuts, bread and most anything so he pretty well had the run of the house.

One morning when we returned to the house after the milking chores, we could smell smoke and after looking in the bedroom where we left "Squirrelly" sleeping in his coat pocket, we found the dresser scarf was partially burned and the top of the dresser scorched and blackened.

Apparently, the squirrel had bit on some matches used to light the kerosene lamp in the bedroom which had started the fire and thankfully had gone out before becoming more serious.

"Squirrelly" was nowhere to be seen but we knew he had been in the bedroom with the door shut. After looking all over, we finally found him buried in the dirty clothes hamper with both his front paws over his eyes like he was afraid he would be punished for what he had done.

Because there had been other possible problems with a squirrel in the house, we decided to keep him outside which wasn't easy. He'd be waiting on the roof above the door for anyone to let him in by jumping down on their shoulder or head (which was pretty scary for any stranger).

Gradually, he spent less time trying to get in and more time with other squirrels. When winter came, most squirrels hibernated during real cold weather and lots of snow and we wondered where our squirrel could be?

In the spring while feeding the last of the hay out of the hay-mow, I found a bushel size ball of corn husks, corn silk, and leaves with a hole in the center and I was pretty sure that's where "Squirrelly" had spent the winter but we never saw him again.

It doesn't seem to matter what the specie may be, when you love animals and care for their well being, you are going to have stories to tell for a very long time. This tale is over seventy years old and still makes me smile when I think of that little creature lurking on the roof waiting for the human "bus" to come along so he can go inside and be warm.

CHAPTER 8

LADY'S SECRET

Sandy and Carl Tegtmeir of Battle Lake, Minnesota are real animal lovers who have had their share of lovable lap dogs and crazy kitties. This tale isn't about squirrels as much as it is about a dog obeying her master... kinda.

In 1989 my husband, Carl, and I purchased a 7-1/2 year old German Shepherd Dog. Lady filled our lives with love and laughter for another 7-1/2 years. This is a "Lady" story.

When Carl was walking our dogs one day, a squirrel missed a branch and met his demise. Our dogs pounced before Carl could stop them. Lady claimed this prize but Carl told her to drop it. She complied but later she went back to retrieve her trophy. Carl sternly told her to leave it, adding "I don't want to see it again."

Later, when I was walking the dogs, Lady picked up the squirrel and brought it home. She was so proud of it I let her keep it, even though I knew Carl had asked her to leave it. When we got home, Lady stashed the squirrel in her dog house. If I took her for a walk, she brought her squirrel. If

Carl took her, there was no sign of it. If she had the squirrel when Carl came outside or drove into the yard, she'd stash it in the nearest snow bank or in her doghouse.

Carl tried to catch her with her squirrel but she was too quick. He never did see it again I finally disposed of it and ended the game. We had a lot of laughs over how resourceful she was.

Lady has been gone for years but we have lots of memories of her antics. We are also sharing our house with our fourth Shepherd... we can't outwit her either.

I had a battle of wits with the squirrels before my shepherds arrived. My stepson, Jacob, likes to tell us he remembers when we first bought the property, we gushed on and on about how cute the squirrels were. As the year wore on and our patience began to wear off, he said we started to change our tune. The first winter took me outside on cold morning in a robe with a BB gun trying to scare the bushy tailed rats away from the bird feeder. My wife continues to say to this day that I looked a little crazed.

Try as I may, the BB gun just wasn't accurate enough. It seemed the squirrel would jump into mid-air and run for his life but after a while; they got used to the BB pellets and basically ignored the slight discomfort they produced. A .22 was next. I have trouble convincing my wife that I qualified as a sharpshooter in the service because I shot up "her" bird feeder attempting to eradicate the squirrel population. How was I to know that an Oriole feeder would just jump out at me like that one did? I shot it in self defense.

These days, the squirrels come and go as they please and seldom come near the feeders like they did before. The dogs chase them up a tree now and then just to keep them on their furry little toes. The rabbits are a different thing altogether... they have made gourmet dining a daily affair in our gardens. Much to my wife's chagrin, I have promised on more than one occasion to eradicate them with my trusty .22 rifle. They seem to know just when the dogs are locked up and then they come out to pillage our tasty garden treats.

I can easily imagine the odiferous emanations coming from a pot of rabbit stew (because I'm the chef in the household) but as I said before... Cindy will make sure it stays in my imagination. She has such a tender heart for almost all animals that I bow before her kind considerations (meanwhile they are munching away in the night).

CHAPTER 9

THE DAY OF THE POSSUMM

When you live with cats long enough, it seems like they can talk to you. Fritz used to convey his desires to me with that patented "raaaant" and usually there was something going on of which I was unaware and he would bring it to my attention.

As I have stated before... I am a dog person. Until Fritz, I tolerated cats as most dog people do: within reason. In a divorce, the Ex got the bulk of our community property; I got the jazz collection and Fritz. I got the better deal. I bought her this lovable little fur ball kitten who happened to be a pure bred blue Persian. I brought the kitten home and she went shopping for four hours; consequently while feeding and taking care of young Fritz, we bonded... quite well I might add.

Because Persians have that squashed face, they sometimes have defects in breathing or in their jaw line. Fritz had a slight twist to his lower jaw and when he closed his mouth, a tooth would protrude forth. When he closed one eye, cocked his head, and looked directly at you, he looked like a pirate. You could almost hear him say, "Aye me hearties."

As the years passed and Fritz grew and grew and grew (finally stopping at seventeen pounds) he never became the docile house cat with that hoity toity attitude, he was an outside cat that chased large dogs. In fact I raised and trained him like a dog. As Fritz and I grew older together, he never stopped amazing me with his cunning, intelligence, and shear strength and on one particular afternoon, his dedication in bringing me a present... a live trophy mind you.

I was sitting on the couch enjoying a rare moment of leisure watching a baseball game. I heard Fritz come through the cat/dog door in the kitchen. He usually got a drink of water and then made his presence known shortly thereafter. The sound of claws or toenails on linoleum summoned my attention to the doorway between the living room and the kitchen. I nearly fell off the couch in astonishment.

A full grown female (or male) possum was scurrying straight for me looking for a way out of the house and away from Fritz, who at the time was caterwauling at the top of his lungs. I think it was a female because three days later he drug a younger adult possum through the cat door again.

Now I don't know if he drug momma through the door but he definitely kidnapped (or is it possum napped) the youngster. I still can see him sitting there grinning that pirate smile. I had him for eight and a half years before a kidney disease took him. I smile when I reminisce about all his adventures. I cried like a baby when I had to put him down.

When cats become house pets, they take on a slightly different attitude than their outdoor cohorts. They take on certain attributes that are normally identified in humans. I'll let Shirley Johnson, of Battle Lake, Minnesota, tell her tale.

My husband, Sherman and I have a cat named TROUBLE. My grand daughter calls her the "Trouble Cat" and she is a tattle cat.

Recently, I asked my husband to please remove the papers, magazines, etc. Off the coffee table. When I arrived back home everything was clean as a whistle. I sat down to watch TV and here comes TROUBLE (by the way that's how she got her name) and she greeted me and immediately went over to the second couch and started pawing between the cushion and the couch. She would then come over to me and I asked her what she was doing? She did this a few time so I decided to investigate. I looked under the cushion, and you guessed it, there were the papers.

My husband arrived home later and I thanked him for cleaning. I said I know where the papers are. He said, "You do not". I went over and pulled up the cushion. You should have seen the look on his face. I said TROUBLE had tattled on him and he could hardly believe it.

We acquired TROUBLE by calling a found ad in the paper and asking them what they would do if they couldn't find the owner. They couldn't keep her and we took her with the understanding that we would give her back if the owner showed up. She did, and we were so afraid we would have to live up to our obligation, but the owner just wanted to make sure she had a good home and that made my husband, myself, and TROUBLE very happy. That was twelve and one half years ago and we have loved her ever since.

Be careful folks, our pets can "rat" us out like the felonious inmates in a state prison. They are family... maybe more like kids than adults, though.

CHAPTER 10

TOMMY

One of the tales I received came all the way from Arizona and this one takes the cake for being rather incredible. I still shake my head trying to figure out how and why Tommy is still alive. If you don't believe that cats have nine lives, maybe you should read this tale closely. This tale is from Mary Evenson Hubbard of Green Valley, Arizona and she spins a yarn (no pun intended...ok, maybe a little bit) you'll be sure to appreciate.

A few years ago we adopted Tommy, a beautiful big gray and white (neutered) tom cat from the local animal shelter. He turned out to be a wonderful pet in ALMOST every way.

Shortly after he settled in to his new surroundings, we discovered his love of eating thread. I am an avid quilt maker and every evening I would sit down and hand quilt until it was time to turn in. My habit was to thread the needle for next time and wrap it around the spool and leave it sitting on the table by my chair.

The next evening when I sat down to sew, the spool of thread was on the carpet and the needle and thread were GONE! I searched frantically everywhere and there was no denying it, Tommy must have eaten it. I called the vet and made an appointment for an x-ray. There it was, as clear as could be on the x-ray about two thirds of the way through his colon.

I was told by the vet that he would probably pass it within twenty four hours. If not, I was to bring him back and he may have to do surgery to remove it. Thankfully, that evening, "everything" came out all right. End of story? No, not quite!

I bought a box with a spring loaded lid on it to keep my thread and needle in. I thought that would be very safe as, although I knew Tommy was pretty smart, he would not be able to open a box like that. That evening when I returned home from work, the box was on the floor, the lid open and, you guessed it, the needle and thread were GONE!

This time we decided to save the one hundred fifty dollar x-ray and just wait it out and keep checking the litter box. On about the third day he returned the needle and thread to me in somewhat of a "used" condition... if you get my drift.

Well, I have finally learned my lesson. WRONG! About a year later a friend came over with her embroidery as we were going to do some sewing together. She laid her sewing down on the coffee *table and when we sat down to sew, she thought she had threaded three needles but she could only find two. I said she must have been mistaken but in the back of my mind I knew I would have to start carefully checking the litter box again for the next few days.*

Tommy returned this needle also but my friend really didn't care to have it back! It happened one more time but this time he threw it up in a nice big fat hairball. Dodged another bullet!!

I figure Tommy has only five of his nine lives left so I am really being careful these days. He still unthreads my sewing machine every time I turn my back and comes running from the other side of the house if he hears me tearing fabric. He knows there will be some very exciting threads to grab.

I read her letter twice... making sure I didn't miss anything. It shouldn't be possible for a cat to swallow something that sharp and not puncture anything. I find it truly amazing but not once but four times? That's incredible. That's the joy of having people send in their stories, you find real nuggets like Tommy. Of course, you can never tell what is just around the corner. Can You?

CHAPTER 11

SMOKIN'!

They say curiosity killed the cat. That certainly can be true in some cases but I have found that there is almost always, an exception to the rule. Curiosity found a delinquent dad's hidden papers; it helped a male cat use up four of its nine lives, and in the case of Benson... it produced fire.

In the case of Sara Keysor, trouble can be lurking just around the corner; or in this case... right at the end of the couch. She is a much wiser person these days... let's hope Benson is.

Sara worked at the PAAC (Perham Area Community Center) front desk when our paths crossed last year... she also taught early childhood in Frazee. Sara Keysor is a person with whom people have trusted their children and is a very capable person. All in all, she is a very responsible woman who shows a lot of courage in telling me that she set her cat on fire. Well, she didn't exactly set the cat on fire... the kitten did all the pyrotechnics itself... Sara had just a lit candle in striking distance.

Maybe I should start in the beginning. One night Sara was watching TV with her young precocious kitten "Benson". Being seven months old, Benson was the epitome of kittenhood... rambunctious and into everything. It seems Sara had a scented Glade candle burning away on the end table next to her. The room smelled terrific. Young Benson found this to his liking and approached the candle to inspect its odiferous qualities himself. He thought it smelled good too. Since Benson was a domestic long hair cat and he, of course, had a long bushy tail that swung back and forth like a furry pendulum. Need I say more about the inevitable?

The program on the tube must have been very engrossing because Sara didn't notice her cat's tail on fire until she smelled that unmistakable odor of burning hair. You can imagine what she must have thought to see good ole Benson headed for the bedroom with his tail on fire. She sprung from the couch like a sprinter leaving the starting blocks and tackled the young feline on the run. With tail alight, and his mistress flailing away at his rear quarters, the kitten was scared to death... well not quite but she tells me he wasn't quite happy with her at the moment.

The fire was extinguished and Sara and her not so furry feline were reconciled after a lot of coaxing and loving treats. To this day, his tail isn't the round tapered one before his accident; it's a little squared off at the end. He doesn't seem too traumatized by the incident but I bet he stays away from open flames.

With all this said, it only goes to show that no matter how responsible you are and how careful you tend to be, pets can find trouble on their own. They can get into garbage cans and get sick or eat something that they shouldn't. This is all a part of pet ownership. What can we do to prevent these things from occurring? We can be vigilant and pay close attention to everything they do (which is next to impossible) or we can make sure that their environment is safe by observing what could be detrimental to their health. This requires a little common sense and awareness to your pet's needs.

Sara thinks she was negligent that night but in reality, she really wasn't. She has since moved the candle out of the reach of her buddy Benson and they live in relative comfort... just waiting for curiosity to raise its semi scorched head (or in this case, its tail). That is the nature of living with our unpredictable pets. You never know until it happens.

CHAPTER 12

THE UNPLEASANT PHEASANT

Cats can get into trouble with hardly any effort at all it seems. Puppies most assuredly can be a handful when left to their own devices. What do you say about a pheasant that looks for trouble? This one goes out of his way to cause a ruckus. All the pheasants I've come in contact with over the years have been quite shy of people... especially those carrying loaded weapons.

Ike Fischer has been a regular contributor to the tales column and here's another one from the man from Frazee, Minnesota. His life has been a collage of many events and adventures that lend themselves to the re-telling of them. I'm thankful for his input (us writers have to stick together). Here's a tale I'm sure Ike has told more than once... attack pheasant stories just don't come along everyday.

I used to raise a lot of pheasants to turn loose hoping to increase the wild population of birds to hunt, but unfortunately the animal, bird, and human predators kept depleting the birds as fast as I released them.

Pheasant roosters are very territorial and will fight

each other or most anything else daring to enter their territory. My nephew had a three wheel ATV with large soft tires that he used to check the cow/calf herd in the pasture and one rooster began trying to chase the intruding machine out of his range He kept getting closer and more daring that he finally was hit and run over with the soft tires.

Unhurt, it just made the rooster madder and it began attacking any machine that came by; especially a car that would blow its horn which resembled the crowing a rooster did to proclaim their territorial rulership. If we parked a car and blew the horn, the rooster would come on the run or fly up on the vehicle's hood and glare into the windshield. If we turned on the wipers, he would try to grab them with his bill.

One day a couple drove by on a motorcycle going south, then turned to come back and the rooster flew out of the bushes beside the road to "attack" the invading cycle. The surprised couple tipped their cycle over on its side with considerable cursing and tried to "shoo" the angry rooster away which wasn't about to give up until they left... then the rooster flapped his wings and crowed in victory.

When hunting season arrived we were sure he'd be an easy mark for an eager hunter, so we captured him and put him in a pen with the hens we kept over the winter. He became despondent, mostly just sat around and sulked, feathers getting dirty and ugly. So when hunting season was over, we turned him loose again. He let out his usual war-whoop and flapped his wings.

About then, the school bus drove by and the rooster took off after it. Kids on the bus said he was still chasing them a mile or so later and we never saw him again!

I can see a wanted poster with that rampaging rooster's picture on it. WANTED DEAD OR ALIVE. You can learn something new about wild animals every day if you want. They are truly amazing.

CHAPTER 13

THE DAY AND NIGHT OF THE DRAGON

In this day and age, it seems almost every animal on the planet is on the endangered species list. Don't get me wrong, I believe in being the best steward of animals as I can be but some things can be carried too far. It's true that humans are the most prolific predator but even the lofty man in all his glory and intellectual superiority can fall prey to the right beast... and in doing so; becomes an endangered specie himself.

I was first introduced to this particular endangered specie on a deserted beach in Viet Nam three months prior to the fateful night I shot another one on guard duty. That's right... I confess. I shot and most likely killed an endangered specie in 1967. Okay, it probably wasn't endangered at the time (other than from scared soldiers with guns) but none the less it got shot. I'm getting ahead of myself again... let's start at the beginning.

It was the fourth of June, 1967 and Cam Ranh Bay, Viet Nam in the summer was swelteringly (hope this is a word because that's what it was) miserable. I was in country only three days. They put the "newbies" (cherries) on guard duty because they didn't know what else to do with them. A newly found friend from a nearby town back in California and I had just gotten off all night guard duty and we asked if there was a beach nearby. Looking to catch a few rays, snooze a bit, and take a dip in crystal clear water, we were directed by a veteran G.I. to a deserted beach. I swear I didn't hear him snicker. Neither did Smitty.

After luxuriating in the morning sun for almost an hour, I turned over from my back to my belly and happened to glance down the beach. I blinked a couple times. I wasn't sure of what it was I was seeing but it was headed directly for us. I shook Smitty to wakefulness and we both grabbed our beach towels and flip flops and clamored to the rise of the nearest sand dune. We had unwittingly invaded the territory of a Komodo Dragon Lizard... the world's largest lizard and much to our chagrin... a carnivore that measures about nine feet long and weighs up to three hundred pounds. I don't know how big our host was but he was getting larger the closer he approached.

Three months later I had acquired Thunder (my jet black German Shepherd) and we were walking a post together around the Long Binh Ammo Dump in the middle of a humid and sultry night that was as black as India Ink. The perimeter had three levels of Constantino wire that had booby traps, anti-personnel mines, and flares attached to it so that if anybody or thing tried to penetrate the wire, all heck would break loose; at least that was the general idea. A road circled the perimeter and the K-9 units would patrol the outside area of where thousands of artillery shells, ammo of all sorts, and a whole collection of pyrotechnics were stored. Did I mention it was really really dark?

As Thunder and I walked our post, one of the tower spot lights that shone out into the darkness sputtered and fizzled and then went out completely. As if it wasn't dark enough, it was difficult to see your hand in front of your face and things from there started to become a little scary.

Thunder froze in his tracks. I stopped, my ears straining for any audible sound. I could hear a scuffling sound in front of us. I had a Colt .45 on my hip and a M-16 slung over my shoulder and a ninety five pound shepherd pulling me toward the sound; his claws digging into the sand with tremendous strength. We weren't together that long and Thunder had a mind of his own and he was in complete attack mode.

I could hear breathing. (Something close to Darth Vader's raspy rattle). The M-16 came off my shoulder and I assumed the defensive posture one takes when they are about to fire. Thunder miraculously stopped on a dime. I shouted, "Dung Lai!" which in Viet Namese means halt. It moved away from us and I shouted once again (with my heart pounding in my ear) probably sounding like Barney Fife. I took aim and fired, no time for any more orders... there were a lot of bombs behind me that I didn't want going off at that particular moment.

The intruder scurried into the Constantino fence and suddenly the night was awash with blindingly brilliant light from flares and booby traps going off one right after another. A machine gun position a couple hundred yards away opened up like it was Omaha Beach. Tracer bullets filled the air.

Collectively, we killed a large Komodo Dragon Lizard... which has poison in its saliva that will kill who or whatever it bites... three days later. Do a Google search if you are interested in the gory details but they are not harmless... whew! And that is how I came to kill an endangered specie and gain the nickname from my buddies... Lizard Killer (or the one I like the best; Dragon Slayer). It took a long time to live that nickname down.

My memories of the time I spent in South East Asia aren't all "war stories" and I choose to focus on the lighter side of those two tours there. General William Tecumseh Sherman said, "War is Hell" and for the Union soldiers of the Civil War he commanded, it indeed was.

The honor that was mine mainly revolved around an animal which had the capacity and ability to save lives with his nose. He was an unsung hero and he had a sense of humor, too. Health regulations prevented me from bringing him home... he would have been a great sire to pass on that incredible intelligence and temperament.

At Fort Benning, in Georgia, there is a war dog memorial that was erected a few years ago. It is a tribute to the ones who never came home; who gave their lives selflessly for their human comrades and their country. I have been and continue to be blessed in many ways in this life of mine... but the honor and privilege to be Thunder's handler will always be on the top of the list.

CHAPTER 14

A HALLOWEEN TO REMEMBER

The summer of 1967 was dubbed as the "Magical Summer" back in California. Long haired "Hippies" and "Flower Children" surged through the streets of San Francisco like a psychedelic river whose banks had overflowed with color. I left for Viet Nam June first (my mother's birthday) leaving the tumultuous throng behind. After acquiring "Thunder" three months later in Saigon, I walked a post with him at Long Binh ammo dump.

Those of you readers who have dogs, here in Minnesota, are surely familiar with heartworm medicine being a major part of your dog's health regimen. The microfilaria mosquito lays eggs in the canine's drinking water thus infecting the poor animal by being virtually undetected by the human eye. Blood must be drawn regularly to be able to identify this deadly culprit. Thunder tested positive for this thread like worm that literally takes over the heart and lungs of the unsuspecting dog, eventually rendering it impossible to breathe. It's a slow and painful death.

It was this condition that brought Thunder and me to Saigon, and it was late October when the daily treatments of an arsenic compound were almost over and we were ready to go back into active duty. John Campbell and Charlie Davis were two handlers whose dogs were similarly infected and were also close to being released from veterinary care. The three of us hung around together and that meant going to town (downtown Saigon) together and having more than a few adult beverages... and we did on that eventful evening... Halloween 1967.

Curfew was twenty two hundred hours (10 P.M.) It could have been twenty one hundred, but I remember (kinda) arriving back at our camp somewhere around 10 P.M. We didn't drive back from downtown Saigon, because only the company driver could transport us in a military vehicle. We were transported by a Lambretta (which is like a combination motorized Rickshaw and a John Deere Gator utility vehicle) whose driver seemed to have a death wish by the way he drove through the city streets. Somehow we made it back relatively unscathed. Our bunks were like a welcoming lighthouse beacon drawing back weary sailors from the sea. We were fast asleep within minutes... but it wasn't to last.

In the heart of Saigon, a very prominent building stands as a veritable fortress unto the night... it is Ky's Palace (the Premier of Viet Nam at the time). Tall rod iron fences with sharp pointed tips jut forcibly into the night's air with a pronounced declaration...

STAY AWAY!!!

Behind these fences standing raptly at attention are mannequin faced guards with nondescript expressions of unmeasured ferocity. Suddenly a blinding flash of light and the immediate vicinity of Ky's Palace is torn asunder with a blast of monumental proportions. The impregnable fortress has been violently violated with a rocket blast. Three dog handlers slept on in uninterrupted bliss... but not for long.

I felt a firm grip upon my shoulder and came out of my slumber with a start. The CQ runner jumped back thinking I was about to throttle his young self. He turned and woke John and Charlie with the same careless abandon...something was definitely up. He told us to be in the Captain's office in ten minutes in full gear; including all necessary kennel equipment. He turned and ran away at full speed. We looked at each other with weary eyes and shrugged ourselves into our jungle fatigues, ammo belts, and secured our weapons from the locker.

When we arrived at the command post, the captain promptly told us that they tried to kill Vice President Humphrey by rocketing Ky's Palace earlier that night... we had to provide security for the Vice President of the United States. We were to go to the kennels, pick up our dogs, and then go to Ellsworth Bunker's French Villa off of Fleur Di Lis Street via three gun jeeps. I almost asked the Captain what were we to say when we got there. Trick or Treat?

Off we went through the streets of Saigon hanging on for dear life as we approached each intersection. After picking up our dogs, we were escorted by some very serious looking G.I.'s in heavily armored vehicles that spoke of serious commitment to action. John and Charlie had the same perplexed expression painted on each of their faces that must have adorned my mighty mug. The enormity of the situation hadn't fully sunk in yet. We were living minute to minute and the news kept getting worse as time flew past us.

As we pulled up to the French Villa, it struck me that this compound could have been on the Riviera or Palm Beach or any other affluent area around the globe. There were high walls manned with men in short sleeved white shirts and skinny black ties. I couldn't help myself; I just had to put my two cents in where I felt it was needed. "Sir", I said to one of the secret service agents that greeted us when we arrived at the scene, "Those are wonderful targets you and your men are wearing, even shows Charlie (the Viet Cong, not my fellow handler Charlie Davis) where center mass is. You might consider O.D. (olive drab) green T-shirts." He growled something about us dog handlers doing our jobs and not to worry about matters that weren't our concern. Then pointed across the street and said, "There is where you should be concerned."

Another shorter rod iron fence encompassed a huge Cemetery...to be exact; it was a French Grave yard replete with cold marble statues and ancient mausoleums. I stood there aghast regretting ever thinking about saying trick or treat. This was NOT going to be a "treat". The back side of the graveyard opened up into jungle... hundreds of yards of indefensible open perimeter where another attack upon the Vice President was a certain possibility. So, off we went into the night walking our happy hounds into who knew what.

Thunder was glad to get out of his kennel and he sensed the excitement of his handler (it was more like fear) and hey guys... it's Halloween. He was up for the moment. John, Charlie, and I were burdened with the task of detecting any attempt at infiltration by the Viet Cong.

Some time around four in the morning, Thunder alerted on a canister partially buried next to a large headstone. I called it in to my superiors and they called the bomb squad (Ordinance Disposal). They arrived and carefully examined the canister. Much to my chagrin, it turned out to be Kim Chee, a very spicy Korean dish that has pork and rice in it and is buried to ferment. So much for my super sniffing sentry dog... he must have thought it was his treat. Thunder was seldom wrong. Even the best of us have an off day.

We finally got our trick and the evening was definitely not a treat by any standard. Once again, humility found me unsuspecting but as we were leaving at the crack of dawn I noticed something that struck me as being very funny.

Every Secret Service agent was wearing a green T-shirt and wore their holsters under their arm...just like us lowly dog handlers. John and Charlie both noticed the change in secret service guard apparel and we each gave each other a knowing look and a smile.

We went back to the kennels; deposited our canines in their welcome abodes, and went back to our bunks and slept the sleep of the righteous.

CHAPTER 15

THE GROWL THAT SHOOK THE EARTH

I took three of my dogs to the Vet one Saturday last year. I breed pure bred German Shepherds so it's very important to stay on top of their health issues. Dr. William Rose has treated all my dogs for going on four years now and he said he was in the most peril when drawing blood from my one hundred twenty pound female (Lara Mee has gained weight since being pregnant). He didn't fear those jaws that have ripped chain link fencing apart; nor did he bid caution against the travails of that gigantic tail. He was face to face with that tongue. Yes, the one that could cover your entire face with one sloppy slurp. In my mind, there was a question that begged to be asked.

I asked him about myths and one myth in particular, and that's the one about the anti-septic qualities of the canine's mouth. I wondered if it was true that letting a dog lick your wound would make it heal faster. I'm sure some of you have heard that before. According to Dr. Rose, there aren't any medicinal properties in the dog's saliva that would promote faster healing. There are bacteria in the mouth and enzymes that break down food (particularly meat) faster but they are not considered anti-septic. He said having the dog lick the wound would be better than no attention at all but it is just what it is... a myth.

While there I met a couple bringing their pooch in for treatment. Okay, it wasn't a pooch; it was a beautiful yellow Labrador Retriever. I was asked about shy dogs that cower at the sight of strangers and how to deal with this problem. My advice is this. A dog's temperament is mostly genetic, but their behavior is about training. Hyper pups will be hyper right on through to adulthood but with proper socialization very early, they can be good citizens and not be afraid of everybody who comes along. The owner/handler has the power to mold this fine animal into a loving and well adjusted (but a little bit hyper) adult.

At Rosswood Kennels we get those pups into the hands of adults and children at the earliest time possible; about two week old. Our Momma dog keeps a watchful eye but she knows her kids are safe. In the end, the adult dogs aren't afraid of people and have the temperament we breed for.

Speaking of visits to the veterinarian, I remember a time back in Nam when I had to take my sentry/scout dog to the Vet. Aside from shooting giant lizards, walking around a graveyard on Halloween, a few humorous things did occur during my two tours there. I make it a habit not to tell too many "war stories" but this tale is one that has to be told.

Thunder was jet black, twenty six inches at the shoulder, and had 1æ inch canine teeth (they protruded from his upper lip when his mouth was closed like fangs). When he growled, he curled his upper lip and a set of dentures liken that of the creature from the movie "Alien" was all you could see. Thunder was a very scary looking dog. He had a sense of humor too... he knew how terrifying he looked and would snarl at people just to get a reaction. We were attached to an Artillery unit outside of Nha Trang. Somehow, Thunder managed to get a foxtail down his left ear. The more he scratched at it the deeper it went into the ear canal. He had to go to the Vet; there was no getting around it.

The veterinary tent was adjacent to an area that had heavy foot traffic with soldiers passing by at all times. Getting a ninety five pound dog on a stainless steel table is not an easy chore. Thunder wasn't fond of doctors either. I struggled to get him on the table and after several minutes of head gyrations and obstinate behavior, the Vet had enough. Out came the syringe and a dose of "sleepy bye". It was probably a variation of PCP (animal tranquilizer). The doctor administered the shot and said to bring him back in ten minutes when the medicine was taking hold. Can you see this one coming? Hmmm???

Thunder was sitting by my side as I was squatting down next to him trying to keep him still. I was looking for tell tale signs of his forthcoming drowsiness and wasn't enthralled with the possibility of me having to carry him into the tent and on to the table. Dead weight is dead WEIGHT. My head was close to his right ear and I whispered calming phrases to him.

A GI came strolling along from around the corner and almost stumbled upon us. Thunder growled his obligatory snarl and the soldier jumped back with alarm. With an accent that had to be from "New Yawk" he sneered back a reply, "Is dat one of doz mean killer police dogs? He don't look so mean to me." His arrogance was a bit much for me so I did what any proud dog handler would do. I wrapped my hand tightly around Thunder's collar and whispered once again in his ear with the tone he knew was an alert, "Watch him Thunder."

Thunder tightened against his restraints and rose up on his haunches and bared his pearly white teeth at the petrified soldier. He started to let out his thunderous growl (that's how he got his name) and opened his jaws a little wider and yawned. His tongue hung slack and he fell over into the sand with a resounding thud. We both stood gaping at the unconscious canine. Finally the New Yorker broke the silence. "That's some killer dog you got there pal, hope he enjoys his nap!" Once again, humility can be found at the most inauspicious times and in the most unexpected places!

Thunder

REMEMBERING
THE DAYS OF THUNDER

As the rain pelts down upon my window pane
And the lightning streaks across a purple sky
My thoughts of him flow to the past again
And I know the reasons why

In the keeping of those war time memories
In the days when youth feared no death
A vision of his friendly face comes racing back
to me
His unflagging loyalty had such great depth

Suddenly my room shakes with the sound of
thunder
The ground trembles with each burst
This is no magic spell I'm under
And this memory is not the first

Black as the darkest moment of a moonless
midnight
Thunder was his name
A caring and crafty cautious canine sentry
He should have had great unbridled fame

We found each other in my years of service
We both proudly wore the Army green
One of the four legged warriors who served us
One of the bravest souls I have ever seen

But that wondrous and willing Shepherd
Fell in a silent battle to a threadlike killer worm
His heroic days out in the killing fields assured
That to his homeland he would never return

He stood for all that was true and good
He gave his life up in a very unpopular war
He did all and everything that he ever could
From him we could never ask for more

I salute the unsung canine heroes
Their sacrifices have paved the way
Their memory follows where ever we go
And they are still out there to this very day

Today when I hear it Thunder
When I see the streaks of lightning across
the sky
I think of him with such loving wonder
And a lifelong memory that will never die

Keith Alan Ross
May, 2007

CHAPTER 16

DOG DAYS PAST AND PRESENT

As I sit down to write my columns, it seems I'm always fending off my rather large (one hundred twenty pounds) female German Shepherd, Lara Mee. There is a battle of wills being fought as I attempt to create and convey my tales. Self petting is when she thrusts her head under my hand and nods up and down. I don't have to do anything but keep my hand steady. It's hard to type when she does this but I manage. I have learned to grab her collar by my left hand and type one handed (not one fingered) while holding her at bay.

Now she has learned a new trick. My computer chair has rollers and Lara Mee leans into me as I'm typing one handed and I slowly drift away from the keyboard with her nuzzling me into the next time zone... ok, it is just about six feet but I still can't reach the keys. She gets plenty of attention and affection every day but her definition of "plenty" and mine are diametrically opposed it seems.

She has also learned to open the door to go outside and has learned to open the door from the outside going back in. To do this maneuver requires a certain amount of dexterity that I didn't know she possessed.

To illustrate just how smart she is, she plays dumb if we are standing by the door waiting for her to open it. She looks up with those big brown (I'm going to eventually get my own way) eyes and waits until we relent and open the door we all know she can open herself.

It's all about that unconditional love we receive from our pets. They don't care what we are wearing, the color of our hair, the type of car we drive, how much we make, or our status in the community. Can you imagine having a human friend like that? If you do, you are very lucky indeed. They teach us so many things about loyalty, trust, and faithfulness.

Speaking of which, I have a tale from Ed Krause of Ottertail, Minnesota that addresses this very subject. I had the pleasure to meet Mr. Krause in person recently and he is a treasure trove of memories and untold tales. Here's Ed's tale about days gone past.

My Dog Story

I have enjoyed reading the stories written about man's best friends; about our faithful dogs. I think most of us have had a special pet that we enjoyed in our lifetime. I was born and raised on a farm in North Dakota. We always had a dog; a dog was a necessity to help manage the cattle as well as a watch dog and a friend. No one drove into our yard without the dog letting us know about it.

When I was a baby, my folks answered an ad that was in the 'Farm Magazine': "For Sale Black and White Male Shepherd Puppies." They sent for one. It came in a box through the Post Office. They named it "Shep".

Shep grew up to be a very smart and helpful dog. My mother tells of an incident when I was about two years old. I was outside with my sister and they didn't know where I had gone; they didn't see me around and they looked and couldn't find me. My mother noticed Shep was acting strange so she told Shep to find me. Shep led her to me. I was lost and crying. Shep was the hero.

Shep always barked when a car drove into the yard. We always knew when someone was there. If someone was different looking or was strange to us, he'd make more of a fuss. In the 30's there were peddlers who would come by and try to sell you things This one time in particular, Shep really made a big fuss when they drove into the yard. My mother had quite a time to calling him off.

Two men were selling apples. Their vehicle had an open trunk in the back where they had the boxes of apples and on the roof of their car, they had a chicken crate.

For apples they would take chickens for payment instead of money. They were so persistent that they went to the chicken coop and picked up several chickens and they were going to put the chickens into the crates. My mother insisted that she didn't want their apples, but they would not listen.

Shep was right by my mother's side. She told the peddlers, "If you don't put my chickens down, I'll send my dog on you!" They dropped the chickens real fast and took off down the driveway. Shep saved the day again.

Shep didn't like fire crackers and thunder. If he could, he'd get in the house and hide under the bed. There are so many stories one could tell about a faithful friend like Shep. They are not forgotten; they remain good memories.

I enjoy this tale because Shep and Lara Mee have one thing in common and that is they take issue with thunder and lightning. Lara Mee's jaws have twisted metal to her will and torn chain link fencing like it was cardboard. These are the same jaws that delicately lick her puppies and tenderly place them in a warm and safe place in her whelping kennel. This is the same dog that will knock you down with her tail and then wash your face for you with that magnificent tongue. With a shepherd, you get the full deluxe package of loving and protecting at the same time. I'm sure Ed felt the same way about Shep.

Laredo

CHAPTER 17

A TALE OF OPPOSITES

My German Shepherd sire, Laredo, and I had an opportunity to take part in the Otter Fest Parade one Saturday morning last year, and it was a lot of fun... Laredo loved all the attention from the children we encountered. We were well received by one and all and we're looking forward to doing it year after year.

I need to comment on something before I get to a story from Ike Fischer. This is important. I was impressed with how many children asked permission to pet Laredo. It really encourages me to see parents out there doing a fabulous job of educating their children in the proper way to approach an unknown dog. For those of you, who don't know, let me address this issue in the best way I can.

It's not only proper etiquette for children to ask permission to approach a dog but it is of paramount importance that <u>EVERYONE</u> does this... including all men and women. Failure to do this can get a person bitten. Remember, that these animals are often one person dogs and are very protective of their master (or mistress). Also, asking permission shows respect to the person handling the dog and the dog picks up on that as well. They sense the hostility of an aggressive adversary, of course, but they also hear the tone of a person's voice and key their reactions to that particular sound. When their handler is being treated kindly, they act accordingly. When there is conflict, they resort to their protective nature and all bets are off.

Laredo has the temperament breeders absolutely love and he showed that in the way he observed the close order drill of the Shriner's go carts. His eyes followed them closely but he didn't budge or did he bark. I was so proud of him. I use him as an example because he is excellent with large crowds and for people who have fear based issues of large dogs. I can hear a little voice in my head saying enough bragging about your pretty boy. So, please ask permission to pet another person's dog... with cats; you're on your own.

As with a show dog that has to be under control at all times, the same holds true for retrievers. It's more than difficult to be able to successfully hunt any sort of fowl with a dog you can't properly manage. Ask Ike Fischer of Frazee, Minnesota and he will tell you a tale about a retriever named Buckshot.

Over the years I had several yellow labs, one of which belonged to the owner of a farm next to ours but he lived in town where the dog was always in trouble. So they left him out at the farm where he would get lonesome and come over to our place most of the time so finally the owners said to just keep him.

He loved to hunt with me but had never been trained so he was hard to control. When we would be in a duck blind with decoys and a flock of ducks would fly by, he would jump up or stand on his hind legs to see if they landed in the decoys.

As soon as I would raise my gun to shoot at anything, he would plunge into the water and circle around in the decoy, looking for something to retrieve, even grabbing decoys in his mouth at times...dropping it when realizing it was just a decoy.

One time we were hunting grouse and ducks in the lake region west of Itasca State Park and would park the car and walk through the woods towards Hidden Lakes where there were usually ducks and hunting grouse on the way.

This time my brother was holding Buckshot on a rope while we walked into the lake and were to turn him loose if he heard us shoot. The dog was very excited and unhappy about being left behind and we could hear him barking and howling as we walked towards the lake.

There were some ducks on the lake and we shot

several of them. We could hear him crashing through the brush towards us, barking and howling as he came, then suddenly no more barking.

As he came past us he was dragging the long rope which my brother had been unable to unsnap from his collar in time to release the excited dog. He also carried a rabbit in his mouth that he somehow grabbed along the way... dropping it as he went by on his way to the lake to retrieve any ducks.

There were several there so he circled around them trying to decide which one to bring in. Sometimes he would grab two or three but as he circled the long rope was gathering weeds and soon he was struggling to swim with a couple of ducks in his mouth and a heavy rope full of weeds.

For awhile I thought I'd have to go out in the cold water and rescue my struggling dog but I kept calling and urging him in where he finally made it and after removing the heavy rope, he went back to retrieving the rest of the ducks.

It seems unbridled enthusiasm can not be denied. I watch my dogs in the woods and they run past rabbits going the opposite way. No wonder they aren't used for retrieving. Bunny herders? Now, that's a different question.

Proper training for the specific job you want your

dog to perform is quintessential to any amount of success. In his element, Laredo excels because he is trained to do so. Buckshot excelled in spite of his lack of training. Both followed their true natures. When all else is stripped away, it is the core of the animal that shines forth.

CHAPTER 18

THE EIGHTEENTH STREET SHOW DOWN

I've told a tale about Fritz, my pure bred blue Persian cat I once had who thought he was a dog... well; he was raised and trained like one at least. Here's a story about a time in his life that Fritz might have thought he was a squirrel... at least for a short time.

San Jose, California has a truly wonderful climate year round. It never really gets too hot and never really gets too cold...all terms being relative but for this story, it was a warm sunny morning that ached with idle laziness and reclined in casual slumber. It was a cat's life. Fritz had the luxury of a white picket fenced yard and a gorgeous green carpet for a lawn. When he stretched out his long haired frame of grey feline fur, he was the epitome of relaxation.

Dogs and human beings had to enter through one of two gates and Fritz always had his escape plan... ready for action. His squashed face (which is the trademark of Persians) was twisted in a semi-scowl that should have been a warning to any unwanted interlopers; that even meant for me to leave him alone for the duration of his nap.

I'm not sure how long the war of words had been

going on between Fritz and the large grey squirrel that inhabited the tree next to the yard's side gate. There was significant chatter coming from above and a low caterwauling moan from the master of the yard (which wasn't me).

I stepped up to the security screen door (a regular screen door would have been in shreds within days of our occupation) and looked out to witness this one act play of a war of wills. The squirrel had come down the trunk of the tree maybe four feet from the ground and incessantly chattered insults and other animal expletives that only another four legged creature would understand.

I could see a challenge was being issued forth and to my astonishment, Fritz rolled over and away from the noisy intruder. "What was he up to?" Then I saw the tooth protruding from his lower jaw (a birth defect common in Persians that have that pushed in face) and at that very moment I knew Fritz was laying a trap for his bushy tailed adversary.

Mr. Squirrel ventured down the tree even further and had almost reached ground level when Fritz sprung into action, twisting his body in mid-air and proverbially hit the ground running... towards the gate and the scrambling squirrel who now was racing back up the tree. Fritz catapulted himself off the ground and used the garden gate as a stationary trampoline thus landing him on the tree five feet below the bushy grey tail.

Since I lived in an older neighborhood, underground cabling for phones and television wasn't available... that left the legendary phone line that acted as a bridge across the quiet residential street as the squirrel's escape route (he had one too). Up and around the branches the two of them climbed, with Fritz surprisingly gaining on his prey. Then it happened.

The squirrel was used to springing from tree to tree in his daily ritual of moving about the neighborhood... Fritz on the other hand was not. Mr. Bushy Tail launched himself off what looked like a small twig of a branch and ran for his life across the telephone wire and to the other side of the street; sat up upon the telephone pole and chattered his epithets at Fritz.

He was Fritz the courageous, Fritz the swift, Fritz the cunning who heroically pushed on towards his rival... but Fritz the seventeen pound cat stopped short of the end of the swaying branch bouncing in the gentle breeze. It was there and then he realized he was "Fritz: The Stuck Out on a Limb Cat."

Chuckling to myself, I fetched a ladder from the neighbors and retrieved the caterwauling feline from his embarrassing and delicate position. He might have been thankful for his rescue but he went back to his position on the lawn and glared at the (I could swear that he was smiling) squirrel for the rest of the morning. I never saw the squirrel again... maybe Fritz got closer than he felt comfortable with. Maybe he didn't have nine lives to play with... Fritz still looked to the trees for him for a long time. Maybe discretion is the better part of valor.

CHAPTER 19

BEWARE OF BATHING GYPSIES

In life, I believe, you are either learning or teaching or doing both at the same time. Situations come along that mold you into what you are... if you are receptive to what is being taught at that moment. Some times these teachers are a beloved relative that endows you with wisdom from on high. Other times, it can be our human frailty that bestows the gift of knowledge upon our furled brow. And, as Kaie Buendiger of Richville, Minnesota might tell you... life lessons can be taught by a mare with a propensity for aquatic endeavors. Here's a tale that I just love to tell.

It was mid summer of 1999 and it was hot and humid and just a perfect day to go horseback riding. Kaie has horses of various ages and temperament and she invites friends to go riding with her and sometimes these rides are long and arduous. These trips require more than just a modicum of experience in the saddle and for the average person it becomes quite a challenge.

It seems a friend of hers came down from Alaska to visit and upon his arrival, he professed to be an excellent horseman and to give him the most spirited horse and he would show everybody how great he was in the saddle. I asked Kaie if the word "arrogant" described her visitor from the Klondike and she smiled and said "quite accurately". Have you noticed that I haven't mentioned the horse's name yet?

This lovely mare was named Her Gale Gypsy and was sixteen years old at the time and had quite a personality for a pure bred Arabian. Kaie lived near Underwood on Horseshoe Lake, residing on Pony Road. (I'm not making up these names, trust me.) These equestrian adventures would start at Horseshoe Lake and would arrive at Rush Lake sixteen miles later. The horses and rider would refresh themselves and then head back again. My posterior gets sore just thinking about that much bouncing in the saddle. I don't ride for that exact reason.

It seems our arrogant visitor was just bragging to beat the band about how he had Gypsy under control and what a superior horseman he was when they reached Rush Lake. Gypsy headed straight for the water and drew up on her hind legs like "Trigger" and began splashing water with her forelegs. Mr. Braggadocio was hanging on for dear life when she decided she was in deep enough water to roll over and truly cool off. He went flying one way and Gypsy had herself a good cooling off rinse, undulating back and forth from right to left. With hat in hand he waded back to shore with his brand new boots full of water. Sitting there, pouring water out of the boots, his entire new wardrobe soaking wet, he proclaimed he wasn't getting back on that !@#$%^ horse.

Kaie told me that she informed him it was either walk or get back on the horse that brought him there. He finally got back on Gypsy and I believe the ride back was quieter than the one over. Horses are fantastic animals that are in a class by themselves. Gypsy passed on this spring and she will be sorely missed by all who had to the pleasure to have known her... or even have gone swimming with her.

Sometimes life just seems to deliver social justice just when it's needed the most. I wonder if the life lesson taught here by Gypsy ever got through to our Alaskan horseman. Careful what you wish for and be twice as careful what you proclaim...it may come back to dunk you in the lake of life.

CHAPTER 20

PEDESTRIAN GEESE & FLYING DOGS

Sometimes, things occur right in front of you that need to be shared with others. Betty Kennedy, co-owner of the Station House Restaurant in Perham, Minnesota, was one of several judges in a "best critter tales" contest in the Contact weekly shopper. She couldn't enter this tale for the contest, but she shared it with me anyway and I'm glad she did.

It seems she was in Fergus Falls last year and was sitting in her car near the pond adjacent to the Middle School. If you don't know where it is, it's the one where all the Canadian Geese congregate and tell goose stories to each other. Betty Kennedy swears this is not a wild goose story but a tale about a quite tame and civilized goose at that.

Parked near the pond, Betty observes this particular goose trying to cross the street. After one failed attempt after another to cross the street, the goose finally gives up. It waddles down the sidewalk to the corner and waits for the traffic to let up, then crosses at the crosswalk being very careful to stay within the lines. What a law abiding pedestrian goose it was! I believe if you hang around long enough in life, you'll see some really remarkable things; but you have to be willing to be out there in the world to see them.

Speaking of remarkable things, I had a conversation with Executive Vice President Jeff Lindoo of Thrifty White Drug recently. He had a tale that certainly qualifies. His daughter Megan lives in Minneapolis in a three story condo that has a deck on the roof and this last Easter her Boston Terrier, Owen decided to see if he could fly. Well, actually he might have been the most surprised of all concerned. Let me explain.

Megan and her family and friends were having a BBQ on the roof the Saturday before Easter Sunday and Owen was exploring the confines of the deck... and finding a missing upright in the fence, he slips through and runs towards the edge of the roof. Megan seeing this calls out to him sharply and beckons him back to her but good ole Owen being the sprightly dog that he is, runs faster and hurdles the eighteen inch wall that a lot of old buildings have at the outer edge of their roof. You know what happens next.

Owen is suddenly airborne and luckily there is a tree below him to break his fall... well, maybe slow it down some... maybe not. He hit several branches on his way towards impact but this didn't seem to inhibit his descent. He hit a hatchback vehicle and completely obliterated the rear window and limped away to the open arms of his mistress. Nobody saw the damaged vehicle at that time. Owen was rushed off to the Vet and required some stitches but didn't incur any broken bones.

Upon returning to her home with the injured Owen being treated like the returning king he thought he was, Megan noticed that there was a police vehicle in the back of her building (the scene of the meteoric flight of the terrier from Boston). She discovered that the owner of the damaged vehicle had no clue as to why his car was missing a rear window.

After she told the officer what happened, the mystery was soon solved... well, not exactly. How do you make out a claim for being hit by a flying dog while being parked? Uninsured motorist doesn't quite fill the bill on this one. Good luck in sorting that one out.

It just goes to show what the world is coming to... geese have become pedestrians and flying dogs are filling the air... Go figure.

CHAPTER 21

CHIP TAKES A TRIP

I start all my weekly columns with "Welcome back to the bark side of life" and it has become my trademark or better yet, my theme song (without music) for my endeavors in writing the "Tales". Here is a true tale about an unsuspecting stowaway who relocated from the country to a town. We are going on a journey with Chip.

Back in the winter of 2003, my wife Cindy and I had to go to Frazee and Perham and then back home. The day was bitterly cold and the fell winds of winter pelted us with sleet. I went out to the truck to warm it up (no remote to start the truck up in those days) and I pulled the Dodge around to the front of the house so she could hurry into it without being out in the cold too long.

I waited about ten minutes and sure enough, she hustles to the truck and jumps in. Since we were going to Frazee, I decided to take the back roads and catch state road ten just west of county road eighty right where it leads into Perham. I remember the temperature was somewhere below zero; possibly twenty below zero. The heater in the truck worked just fine and we were toasty warm going down the road minding our own business.

When we got to Frazee, I stopped by Anderson Bus Lines (they do the school buses for Vergas/Frazee School District) to see Tim and I left the truck running. Cindy stayed in the truck. I was in there about five minutes. We were off to Frazee Elementary School where Cindy teaches early childhood classes. This time I waited in the truck for her. See a pattern developing here folks? She was gone about fifteen or twenty minutes.

Finally, she came out and jumped back in the truck and we're off to Perham. Now the wind is howling like a forlorn wolf and the sleet is flying (like Forrest Gump's rain)... sideways. The next stop on this sojourn is Lakeland Veterinary Clinic. This is before they moved to the new location. So we pulled up to the clinic and we both got out.

Dr. Rose wasn't in at that time and we were making an impromptu visit to pick up some meds for the kennels and we returned to the truck within minutes of parking it. Poking his head out from the grill of the Dodge was a chipmunk (I'll call him Chip... not a very original name... I know). The three of us stood there looking at each other; each of us wondering what was going on.

It seems good ole Chip was fond of climbing up out of the cold and up into the engine compartment for his winter lodging. "Wait a second, I thought to myself. Aren't these critters supposed to be hibernating in the wood shed like they normally do?" He continued to look up at us with wonder in his eyes... maybe it was confusion. "Where am I and how the heck did I get here" was written all over his little chipmunk face.

I'm not a cruel person nor am I a tree hugging PETA extremist... but I had a bit of a dilemma. I thought of Chip's family back at Rosswood and how they would miss him. Then maybe he was a bachelor and was in the habit of hitching rides to where ever the vehicle took him.

Before any of these thoughts were allowed to see the break of day, little ole Chip made a mad dash to the nearby shrubbery and disappeared from our sight. That left my pondering academic, for the time being. Another thought came to mind... were there more chipmunks hiding underneath the truck. Did I just commit a Minnesotan version of "The grapes of wrath?" A whole family packed up and transported from one area to another?

We left Chip peeking out from behind a bush and we went on our merry way to complete our shopping and other errands to which needed tending. I hope that Chip made it through the winter... I meant to ask Dr. Rose if he had seen any suspicious looking chipmunks lurking in his bushes but I thought better of it. It's best to let sleeping chipmunks lie.

It became apparent that I wasn't the only transporter of unwitting animals. Ralph Mayer of Ottertail, MN has a tale of his own that might tickle your funny bone...or chicken bone as it was.

CHAPTER 22

THERE'S A CHICKEN IN THE PARKING LOT!

Ralph Mayer of Ottertail City, Minnesota recalls a time when he drove a chicken to work. Huh? Read on!

It really wasn't as great a surprise as it could have been when a co-worker came racing into the printing press room where I was working yelling "Hey there's a chicken in the parking lot!" I cringed in shame! I knew it was my chicken!

A few days earlier, I had to open the hood of my ancient and temperamental Ford pick-up to get it running...as I usually did. A very excited and crabby Bantam chicken exploded in my face as she blasted off a nest that she'd created on one of the large flat areas over the wheels and next to the V8 engine of my very old truck. Lying there on the metal was a couple of tiny Bantam eggs.

I didn't spend a long time marveling at this as those Bantams had been into everything on my place laying those delicate miniature eggs. Even my open toolbox had a broken egg in it coloring my oily wrenches with smelly orange goo. I noticed that our dog often had an orange moustache and her appetite was less than normal. Eggs were found everywhere and shells covered the yard. Our Bantam population had grown into unmanageable numbers in just a few months and the yard was shimmering with the beautiful multi-colored birds.

The large open space under the hood of old trucks attracted a variety of creatures. Mice, cats and now... chickens. Knowing these eggs to be fresh, I gathered them and imagined them in a nice breakfast in the next few days. We had Bantams attempting to cover the earth with their eggs and they and their contributions were often in my diet. They shunned the chicken house that I'd dragged to our farm preferring to nest in trees and lay eggs on tractor seats, garage corners and now the engine of my truck.

With some amount of embarrassment, I admitted to being the owner and several of my co-workers assisted me in running down the brave little mother chicken and placed her in a box along with the couple eggs that were in her truck engine hiding place.

A co-worker looked lovingly at the chicken and eggs and expressed a desire to become the owner of the lot and his wish was immediately granted. I hoped that they'd all be very happy together. I may have offered him several more!

To get there, that bird rode sixteen miles under the hood of a noisy rough riding old truck to protect her eggs. In addition, the exhaust system was probably less than acceptable to be legal and the heat of those old 8 cylinders should have fried those eggs while barbequing the old hen.

I should have shown her more respect!

I think Chip and that chicken must have gone to the same different school together. Who knows what will happen day to day. That's what makes living in rural Minnesota so special... we have no idea what is going to happen next around here.

CHAPTER 23

THE CASE OF THE MISSING KITTY

We've had chickens and chipmunks going for unsuspecting rides down the road, now here's a tale about a cat that went for a ride with the family and went poof... gone! Even Sherlock would have been put to the test on this one. Phyllis (P.J.) Bombadier of Fergus Falls tells a good tale herself. Here's how the cat got out of the bag (car actually).

It was a warm summer morning in 1957. My two children begged to take "Scruffy", our cat, along in the car to get a loaf of bread. So, off all went and upon arriving at the store, (ten blocks from home), I made sure all the windows were cranked up so Scruffy couldn't escape.

Into the store the kids and I went and were in there five minutes at the max. Back to the car (which back in those days we never bothered to lock up) and the kids asked where Scruffy was. We looked around and couldn't see him anywhere. Well, I mused, we'll probably find him under the seats hiding after we arrived back home.

That was not what happened! We searched high and low... Scruffy was NOT in the vehicle! I was beginning to wonder if the kids had even put him in there to begin our trip. Secondly, I questioned the kids about shutting up our car windows, which they assured me they had.

It was just a baffling situation and we decided what had to be...had to be. Scruffy was gone and we knew not <u>WHERE</u>, or <u>HOW</u>!

We opened the back door of our house, loaf of bread in hand, and greeting us from inside was Scruffy! We could not believe our eyes! *HOW COULD HE BE INSIDE THE HOUSE?* Had we never taken him to the store? Even if he could have gotten out of the car, he could NEVER have ran home that quickly; much less open the door, gone inside, and shut the door behind him! My brain was working overtime, trying to sort out the chain of events over and over. The more I tried to rationalize, the more befuddled I became.

I picked up the phone and tried to explain this to my mother. I was doubting my sanity for sure. Then I detected a slight giggle in her voice. She finally admitted she had seen Scruffy in the car at the grocery store and decided it would be fun to pull a practical joke on us. She had taken Scruffy from our vehicle, taken to our home, and left.

It took me awhile to comprehend all this and how it could have happened in such a short span of time.

Mom thought it very humorous but had a hard time convincing me of that. It was a relief for me, though, knowing my mind had not gone berserk after all.

I had a loving and wonderful mother who did stuff like that. A sense of humor is a great thing to have in this day and age of stress and tumult. Sometimes it's not funny. None the less, it makes for an exciting life.

CHAPTER 24

A TRUE TIMEX TALE

I was raised to be gentle with animals and to respect them. Some of us who inhabit this planet of ours must have missed that particular life lesson. It's unconscionable to me that any person would treat their pets (their unconditional loving pets) the way that they do. There truly is evil in the world and sometimes it takes the form of abuse... to others and to their pets.

Rob and Sheila Jacobson of Frazee, Minnesota have a timeless tale to tell... well not exactly timeless. Maybe I should just let them tell their own tale.

Here is the story of how we were picked to be the owners of one large border collie lap-dog.

In August of 1995 my fianc☐ and I decided to elope in Deadwood, South Dakota. We made a two week trip out of it with Deadwood being our first stop. After spending a couple days there we ventured on as husband and wife to Yellowstone National Park and then to Glacier National Park in Montana.

We were on our last leg of the trip, headed back

to his hometown of Devils Lake, ND, where my in-laws lived. (We were living in Detroit Lakes at the time, in between our first and second year of Sign Painting at the Vo-Tech).

We were traveling on Hwy 2 East, about 60 mph, following a pick up loaded with railroad ties that jutted out over the tailgate. All of a sudden my husband, Rob, says, "Look at that puppy." Sure enough, as I looked through the windshield a little black furball was climbing around on these railroad ties, rocking back and forth from the wind. He no more than said, "It's going to fall" and out she went. All we saw was a little bundle of fur going through the air, rolling down the center line with cars veering not to run her over.

Rob immediately pulled to the side and hopped out of the car, as I had to reach over and hit the brake with my foot. He scooped her up and put her in my lap. We watched the pick up she fell from just keep going. The guy didn't even know what had happened! We stopped at a motel that night and gave her a bath and some food. She was ours.

I was trying to think of a name for our little border collie and seeing as we were in Montana, only came up with Huckleberry. Instead, my more creative husband thought of Timex. Since she did, "take a lickin' and kept on tickin'".

We had her checked by a vet when we got to Devils Lake and she had broken a growth plate in her left rear leg but doc said there was nothing really to do about it. She's over 11 years old now and still a puppy at heart. She is the queen of the house and knows it and ALWAYS knows where her ball is!

I sure would have liked to see that man's face when he got to where he was going and no dog in the back. Timex has had a great, spoiled, life and we love her with all our hearts. Someone was looking out for all of us that night.

It warms my heart to know that things worked out so well for that little "furball". I cringe at the sight of a dog in the back of a pickup truck unteathered and allowed to run free in the back. My dogs have a carpet on the bed of our truck and a camper shell on top of that. I usually transport them in a kennel but sometimes I get lazy and let them surf it as I go down the road. Even this practice should be frowned upon but I know how Laredo loves to ride back there. He must have been a Hawaiian surfer in another life.

None the less, we have to be better stewards of our pets because so many animals are injured each year because of owner negligence. I let them ride in the cab of my truck and I feel that is a lot safer for them.

CHAPTER 25

SITTING TALL

George Borgerding of Dent, Minnesota harkens us back to a time when the automobile was still at its infancy and many a trip was taken in them that was an adventure all of itself. Throw in a great hunting dog, and you have a tale. I'll retell George's story in the best way I can.

It was an early Sunday morning in July and the warm weather was in high gear in Melrose Minnesota. The day awaited George and his family like a promise of new and exciting things to come. They were moving to Prior Lake which is thirty five miles south of Minneapolis. Back in 1935, milk trucks were used for many things besides hauling the moo juice to market. They were used to hauling heavy loads and this one was no different.

The furniture was loaded on the well worn truck with care and left hours before the family was ready to leave with what was left of their belongings... somebody obviously wanted a good head start. A four wheel trailer with high side boards was hitched behind the family car and was packed high and tight for the journey which lay ahead.

After double checking every last detail, and packing five kids and a wife into the car, George's father realized something was missing (or should I say some one?) Jack, the Dry Grass Chesapeake, was standing there on the sidewalk with a forlorn face only a dog can muster. What to do? Much to Jack's enjoyment, he was strapped to the top of the belongings on the trailer. His head held high against the wind and his feathered curls flapping in the summer breeze, Jack's family drove towards their new home with happy hearts... until.

Dad remembered something as he drove down the road... 1935 was the first year that towed trailers were required to have license plates... which dad had purchased weeks before. The only problem facing him at that time was the fact that the plates were securely tucked away in the milk truck that had left three hours before. "This could be a problem", George's father ventured to say. The dye was cast and they had to set out and hope for the best.

First they had to get past the Freeport cop which they did admirably. They sputtered down the road with their well packed car loaded with kids hanging out each side and a noble Chesapeake sitting at attention on top of the trailer... the epitome of doghood. Not one officer pulled them over. They were taken with a dog with his nose to the wind, smiling for all to see. All eyes were on Jack. He had the best seat in the house or in this case...on the way to the house. Thank you so much George for a vision into the past. I can see him sitting there just loving the ride. In those days life was simple and pure. Those memories will last a lifetime.

CHAPTER 26

NO BULL

Sometimes I feel like I lived back in the days of World War II from reading those tales about when life was simple and man's word was worth everything. They have been called the greatest generation and I agree most heartedly. There are so many problems today that did not beset the previous generation. There were rascals and con men and all sorts of grifters, but you didn't hear of serial killers or high school shootouts back then. Louis Seiling of Perham tells a story of how he escaped certain death but not for his faithful friend, Patches.

When I was living on my farm I had a dog named "Patches". One day I was working out by my cows, feeding them, when I heard a noise behind me... and here my big bull (about a ton in weight) was coming after me. I ran for the fence, but it was twenty feet from me and there was mud in between.

Any way, the bull got me and knocked me into the mud. All that was sticking out of the mud hole was my head. I still could see his two black eyes over me.

I knew that in seconds I would be under the mud.

I don't think anybody would have found me. I remember saying, "God Help Me". My dog came from nowhere and bit the bull's ear and tore it open. The bull looked up to see my dog, then Patches got a good hold on his nose and hung on. The bull was trying to get him off but Patches wouldn't let go. Meanwhile, I got out of the mud and to safety.

The bull was slinging him around in a circle but the dog did not let go until I told him to. Then I had him chase the bull till he was tired out and then got the bull back in his pen. The next day when I was going to ship the bull out, the trucker said, "I'm not going in there to get him!"

I told him to line up his truck to the door. I put Patches where I wanted him to get the bull out. When the bull was at the right place I said, "Patches, go get him" and he put the bull in the truck... and the bull would never do that to me again.

Lassie always seemed to save the day just at the last second, every week on TV. Louis had the real deal happen to him. They bring us such joy with their love and affection, but how did Patches "know" his master was at the end of his metaphorical rope? They reason things out better than some humans do under the same stressful situations. They can truly be called man's best friend for a reason.

CHAPTER 27

TINKERBELL

I feel that growing up with a pet makes a child more responsible and focused on something other than themselves. They learn about unconditional love from a being that simply adores them for just being themselves. The adoration in a pair of baby brown puppy eyes can melt the coldest of cold cold hearts. They grow into loyal loving pets that could very easily be called "mankind's" best friend.

I did a "best critter tales" contest in the Perham Contact last year and one of the joys of that contest was the entries by the eighteen and younger contestants. I love to see where their young minds are headed and how they reach there literature wise. I want to share a few of tales from some the promising young writers. Here is a tale from ten year old Meribeth Wothe New York Mills, Minnesota.

Tinkerbell is my cat who's been through so much. Her story begins when my aunt asked us if we would like a kitten one day in the spring. We gladly said yes. She is a long-hair tortoiseshell. She isn't exactly "smart" because she was abandoned by her mother and didn't learn the things cats should learn like hunting mice and burying her compost sites.

She didn't learn where the barn was so every morning and night I would put her in there. But, one morning I couldn't find her so I hoped she was still in the barn. When I got back from school I still I couldn't find her. Later that evening the temperature was in the mid 40's and drizzling. We looked and looked but we could not find her. As I called my dog in, I heard a meow. There under the deck was Tinkerbell, as stiff as board. She had hypothermia, so we put her on the heating pad, covered her in blankets, and put a hot water bag on her. When I checked on her about an hour later she was up and walking, a little dizzily, but she was O.K.

Then someone stepped on her hip. She dragged her leg around the house for about a day. I hoped they hadn't broken her pelvis. Fortunately, it was only bruised a little. Another time when she was pregnant she got a cut on her leg that got infected causing her to have her kittens a week early. She wasn't producing any milk, so all of her kittens died. If we hadn't gotten her to the vet in the time we did, she would have died also. But she didn't.

She now rules the house. She tells you everything. She is now caring for her 4th batch of kittens. When the dogs are being annoying sometimes she gives them an open paw, no claws swat. If she doesn't like the food in her dish she yowls loudly. But we love our pampered cat.

CHAPTER 28

THE GREAT ESCAPER

One of the great joys of writing my column is the fact that there are not only good tales out there for the reading but also great tellers of tales as well. They aren't all wizened veteran reporters or adults with fond memories of days gone past... some are prodigies. It is rare to find a young person these days so well equipped with the skills to convey the written word... and do it with humor, self deprecation, and a wit usually found on much older folks. Fourteen year old Nathan Johnson won the "best critter tales" contest with this piece of literary magic... his words like a wand waving in the grasp of the man himself... Harry Houdini. Enjoy!

Hudson Houdini
The Saga of an Escape Artist Hamster

In September of 2006, I bought a hamster. At least, I thought I bought a hamster. Actually, it turns out that I bought Harry Houdini made to LOOK like a hamster.

To the average Joe, Hudson would appear to be a regular old Syrian hamster: sleek, golden fur, short legs, stumpy tail, bright eyes, the works. I know otherwise now. Hudson is a hamster fully capable of getting out of any cage ever designed by a mortal.

The first cage was a Crittertrail One, a cheap cage intended to be a sufficient home for hamsters. Perhaps ordinary hamsters are the only ones that should be in this cage. Hudson, after getting his bearings in the cage, immediately set to work.

In hindsight, I suppose I shall never buy a cage with more plastic than wire, as it may make me a very poor boy. The first time, Hudson gnawed off the latch on his "Petting Zone," a little hideaway at the top of his cage. He popped the lid, and escaped. Luckily, he was still on the roof of the cage when my little brother came in and apprehended him. Back to the drawing board, but not for long.

This time, Hudson crawled up the wire bars surrounding his cage, and popped out the plastic plug that was there only because I hadn't cooked up a neat enough "hamster pipe" rig yet. This escape was a little more prolonged than the first. I didn't notice he was gone until shortly after breakfast. I was terrified that he had escaped in the room where I kept him during the night because of all the noise he made. If that were the case, it would not only take forever to find him, but it would also open him up to the cat.

Once again, my little brother saved the day. We

were looting our room in search of him, when suddenly; Jacob announced that he had found him. He reached back behind a stack of plastic boxes, and hauled out the infamous hamster, dustballs covering him. At this stage of the game, I was beginning to doubt the efficiency of this cage I had. I began to save my cash.

With a dictionary on top of the petting zone, and the plug screwed in so tight I had to get a wrench to open it, Hudson launched his attack on a new part of the cage. He selected the bubble plug on one side of the cage. The bubble plug, like the previous plug, was there for lack of tubular structures, and was the only thing between Hudson and undenied freedom. It was also to his advantage that it was completely housed in plastic. If you've seen the Crittertrail One, you know what I mean. Hudson set to work.

Victory came, fortunately for us, when the whole family was in my room listening to a story. Suddenly, my little sister sat up and said, "Hudson's out!" We looked, and there, magnified in my brother's fish tank, was Hudson! I wasted no time. I grabbed him, thrust him back in, and replaced the bubble plug. Hudson merely pushed it out and got out again. I immediately took action.

A month later, Hudson's resources were a bit limited. The top plug was screwed in tight. The dictionary remained on the petting zone. Electric tape as well as four heavy books kept the bubble plug in. Hudson had one escape left. I noticed that he had begun to chew on the wire, and it never possibly occurred to me that he could get out of there! As usual, I was wrong.

I awoke one night with the vague feeling that I had heard something, like metal on metal. I got out of bed, and went into the laundry room, where Hudson was being stored until morning. To my horror, the door to his cage was open, and he was nowhere in sight. Then, I heard a scuffling in the cat litter box. Yes, this was unused litter. There was Hudson, burrowing.

Furious, I grabbed him up and popped him back in the cage. The next day, we went to Fargo, and I bought Hudson a glass aquarium. If he got out of this, I was throwing in the towel. He did. He crawled up the water bottle, and got out the top. But his crowning glory was yet to come.

One morning, I awoke and went to move Hudson back into my room. Hudson was gone. I couldn't believe it. I had even put a towel over the top, stupidly thinking it would keep him in. The door to his room had been open for hours, so the cat could get in and get food. He wasn't in the litter, the litter box, or anywhere in the laundry room. We shut all doors, placed the cat in solitary confinement until the convict was located, and dug out the sunflower seeds. Then, it occurred to me that there was one place in the laundry room that we hadn't checked. The reason for a laundry room!

We pulled out the ironing board and laundry basket. There was a gap at the back of the washing machine, easily big enough for the conniving rodent to get into. I knelt down, and heard the distinct sound of gnawing. For a brief instant, I had a fleeting and horrifying image in my mind of Hudson, up in the innards of the washing machine, gnawing on vital working parts. Quickly, Dad tilted up the washing machine, a feat harder than I made it sound, and there, underneath the washing machine, chewing a cheeked piece of corn, was Hudson! Thank heavens.

A short while later, I purchased a wire and metal top for the aquarium, made specifically to fit aquariums of Hudson's size. He hasn't escaped since. Well, okay, let me rephrase that.....he hasn't escaped YET.

Having a hundred twenty pound escape artist myself, I can truly appreciate the quandaries in which Nathan found himself. The cunning and guile of those creatures who, for many years uncounted, have been considered "dumb" is enough to keep the best of us on our toes. Good Job Nathan. I think we'll hear from the young man some day. Don't be surprised if he isn't a best selling author before it's all over.

I also received a tale from a fourteen year old young lady from New York Mills, Minnesota and she wrote in about an animal that displays a lot of "reasoning" skills on a daily basis. Here is Julie Eisenlohr's tale about a "Shadow" that follows her around.

THIEF

We have a pet ferret who is white and gray: his name is "Shadow". My dad got him from my brother for Father's Day. I wanted to write this story about him because it makes me laugh every time I think about it.

So anyway, the story is a couple weeks after we got him, we bought a bag of potatoes. We put the potatoes on the floor. You see, Shadow runs freely all day MOST of the time. When we went to town the next day, we came home and we were going to make potato salad. We went to get the potatoes but there weren't any. We thought maybe we didn't buy any so we went back to town and got some more.

A couple days later the remote control for the TV went missing. Then one day I was cleaning my room and I had the door open and Shadow came and he took a ball and ran down the hallway. So I followed him. He went under my parent's bed, so I flipped the bed spread over and pulled a blanket out and here was the remote, all the potatoes, and the ball.

When we buy potatoes or use the remote, we have to be careful where we place it or it might end up missing. We give Shadow a lot of bouncy balls to play with and he is truly a great Pet.

It only goes to show that when you live with (wild) animals, things literally can get pretty wild. I recall Glen Lutz's raccoon was quite a conniver as well so this ability to reason things out isn't just limited to cats and dogs. The whole animal kingdom all seem to possess some level of advanced intelligence... but isn't that why we love them?

CHAPTER 29

THE ICE ANGEL

Marlo Henneman's, of Fergus Falls, Minnesota granddaughter, Emily, wrote this tale and it is remarkably very similar to an incident we had here at Rosswood. The northern plains are blasted by wicked winter winds that put many a person in peril every year. Blizzards are deadly and people arm themselves against those rigors with emergency kits that sustain them through the ordeal.

What do our precious four legged friends do when faced with life and death situations? They cannot tell us what is wrong or who is in harms way. Can they?

It was a long cold winter but Rommel, a very large Rottweiler and Gidget, an English Staffordshire Bull Terrier were outside playing. They liked to chase each other and bark. Rommel had remained a puppy all his life but Gidget acted more grown-up. Rommel saw a bunny going across the ice and went after it but he was so heavy that he fell through the ice.

Gidget didn't cross the pond. She never went where she could see ice. She was a sensible dog. She went back to Jake & Marlo's house, the place

141

where she was visiting. They were Rommel's owners. They didn't see Rommel around, so they searched & searched but didn't have any luck in finding him. Gidget spent the night on Rommel's bed playing with his toys, which was weird because she never liked toys before.

The next morning Tim, their grandson came & helped look for Rommel, who was very cold because he had been in the water overnight. He could not bark to tell them where he was because of the freezing water & mud was up over his neck & it paralyzed his vocal cords. Tim looked and looked in all the wrong places, but Gidget remembered where Rommel fell in and led Tim to him.

Tim & Jake pulled Rommel out and wrapped him in blankets and took him to the vet. He was not hurt but very cold and would have died that day if Gidget hadn't told Tim where he was. Gidget was the hero of the day.

A few years later Rommel died after a long battle with bone cancer. He is missed very much by his family and Gidget, of course. But we will never forget that cold day that Gidget saved Rommel. She is the family angel & was sent to us for a reason. Rommel never did learn his lesson. He loved water & chasing bunnies all his life.

He is in dog heaven now and Gidget is enjoying a

well deserved life with her family at a lake near Ashby. To this day she does not like water and ice. She loves her family and she did love her buddy, Rommel. She misses him like we shall see him again one day.

I don't know if Emily had ever heard of Rainbow Bridge when she wrote that lovely testament to a beloved pet but she sure was on to something. As Paul Simon and Art Garfunkle once sung so eloquently, "Like a bridge over troubled water, I will lay me down." Pat (Trish) Herder sent me this piece. The author of this tome is unknown but the sentiment will live on forever. Thanks Pat!

RAINBOW BRIDGE

Just this side of heaven is a place called Rainbow Bridge. When an animal dies, that has been especially close to someone here, that pet goes to Rainbow Bridge.

There are meadows and hills for all our special friends, so they can run and play together. There is plenty of food and water, and sunshine, and our friends are warm and comfortable.

All animals who have been ill and old are restored to health and vigor; those who were hurt or maimed are made whole and strong again, just as we remember them in our dreams of days and times gone by. The animals are happy and content, except one small thing; they each miss someone very special to them who had to be left behind.

They all run and play together, but the day comes when one suddenly stops and looks in the distance. Her bright eyes are intent; her eager body begins quivering. Suddenly, she begins to run from the group, flying over the grass, her legs carrying her faster and faster.

You have been spotted, and when you and your friend finally meet, you cling together in joyous reunion, never to be parted again. The happy kisses rain upon your face; your hands again caress the beloved head, and you look once more into the trusting eyes of your pet, so long from your life but never absent from your heart.

Then you cross Rainbow Bridge together...

Young Emily was definitely on to something.
Out of the mouth of babes...

CHAPTER 30

THE CHRISTMAS MOUSE

I once said that dogs have a sense of humor but cats know how to get even and better yet; get their own way. This requires more than a modicum of cunning and guile and reasoning skills. As they say, revenge is a dessert that is best served cold.

Connie Sanders of Perham, Minnesota has a Siamese female that is used to always getting her own way... well, almost always. She does know how to get revenge, though.

Sam loved Christmas... the ribbons, the bows, and best of all, the ornaments with bells; all placed at the bottom of the tree just for her. Sam also loved to chase mice. She was a terrific mouser and often presented the trophies to me. So I wasn't surprised when she walked into the living room with a mouse. What did surprise me was when she walked to the fireplace, put the mouse down and gave it a bath! Then the two snuggled together by the fire.

For the next three days, the two were inseparable. They played together, roamed the house together and always ended up sleeping by the fire. I became quite fond of the little mouse myself and twice, fearing for its safety, carried it to the woodpile in the back yard where his family lived. Both times the little fellow scampered back across the snow, slipped under the house siding, and before I could get my coat off... the two were sleeping by the fire!

On Christmas Eve day, I saw Sam go upstairs... the little mouse went to the kitchen, down the basement stairs and out. The last I saw of him, he was running across the yard to the woodpile to spend the holiday with his family. He had plenty of stories to tell.

Was it the spirit of Christmas? No doubt about it. In our house that Christmas it was, "Peace on Earth- Good will to mice and men"! It was a magical Christmas that I'll never forget... thanks to Sam and her Christmas mouse. Oh yeah... after the holidays, Sam was a terrific mouser.

Why do natural born enemies bond together like that? There are things in this life and times that defy logic... hmmm? Could it be that Sam needed a holiday from chasing little mousies? There was definitely some reasoning going on there. The next saga deals with retribution. See if you agree that there was a concerted effort to make a point by the sagacious Sam.

VENGEANCE...THY NAME IS SAM

As I stated before, Sam loved Christmas. There were exceptions to this. She hated it when I went on vacation and left her home alone. And, she always found a way to let me know.

This particular Christmas, I had put up a small four foot tree on a table by the window. The decorations were pretty and Sam seemed to enjoy them. On the day I left, I picked her up and told her I loved her and would be home soon. I also asked her to "please leave the tree standing for me".

A few days later I returned. Sam met me at the door and seemed happy to see me. When I saw the tree still on the table, I praised her for leaving it in one piece for me. With that said, she gave me a look that could have dropped an elephant in its tracks! She walked over to the tree, and with one well placed swat, knocked it to the floor. Then she calmly walked away.

There are those who say animals can't think or reason but only act on instinct. These people didn't know Sam. She thought this out for several days and plotted the best way to let me know that this was no accident. She meant it! Lucky for me, Sam didn't hold a grudge and we were soon enjoying each other's company once more.

Well, was there clear evidence that Samantha used her reasoning powers to exact revenge on the recalcitrant Connie? I know cats plot against their masters and mistresses when things aren't going their way. Like I've said before, dogs have a sense of humor but cats know how to get even.

CHAPTER 31

CHOIR PRACTICE BEGINS

Here's a tale about how the Rosswood Kennels all girl choir got its name. An all dog choir you ask? Yep! Let me explain this one so you can truly understand why we say we live on the bark side of life here. You have already read that four and one half years ago we purchased several pure bred German Shepherds to begin our breeding program. One of these females was the infamous Lara Mee who now weighs close to one hundred twenty pounds. I was told that she was a kennel wrecker when we purchased her. Being a former dog trainer in the Army (and being blessed with a moderately big male ego), I said no problem. I can handle her. Yeah right! Remember all those humility lessons that I have written about throughout the years? They still are being taught here at Rosswood.

My step son, Jacob, is a builder and a mighty fine one at that. He built me a very strong and functional kennel behind the house and together we put the kennel panels together. They are the ones that look like chain link fencing. It was a thing of beauty. Upon her arrival, Lara Mee was locked in her new abode and I went to town for more supplies thinking that things were just hunky dory (I love that phrase).

We had also acquired another female named Gracie (as in say good night) and she occupied the kennel next to Lara Mee. They seemed to get along at that time. Operative word is "seemed" here folks. The future held some unexpected surprises for us. I left the two of them with happy faces and tongues hanging from their mouths in rhapsodic splendor. Everything was (can we all say this together?) hunky dory.

My wife was home doing something creative on the sun porch which occupies most of the front of our house. I was gone maybe a total of fifteen minutes when I get a call on my cell phone. It seems our kennel wrecker had lived up to her reputation. Cindy had a visitor in the form of our Lara Mee. I hurried home to find my wife in the company of not one, but two female shepherds. Gracie made her disapproval of being left alone in her newly found home quite loudly. Cindy, being the ultimate peace maker, let her out and both ladies vied for her attention in the most urgent manner.

I surmised the situation as somewhat comical but that feeling wasn't as enthusiastically shared by my lovely wife. I inspected the kennel next and found the chain link torn away in one corner like it was paper. There are metal slats that hold the chain link together and one of them was bent like the letter J. Properly trained sentry dogs in the Army can generate up to one thousand pounds per square inch in their jaws. It's only that kind of power that can literally bend metal.

I set to re-enforcing the kennel with heavy duty chain that was interlaced through the chain link. I added support with U bolts and surprisingly enough, it did the trick. I had both the females back in their newly repaired homes when something very odd happened. Cindy was standing next to me and she can confirm what happened next did indeed happen. Lara Mee walked over to the panel that separated her and Gracie and looked directly into her eyes.

Lara Mee's head bobbed down once, then once again, now being joined by Gracie who was imitating the same gesture. It was like a band leader counting off the beat for the orchestra to follow. On the count of three they were in perfect unison, both heads bobbing together. Then on the fourth down beat they raised their heads together and began to howl... not really a howl but more of a baying like a coon hound or a beagle.

In all my years around shepherds, I have never witnessed them baying (much like the hound of the Baskervilles) in two part harmony. Two or three minutes passed and there hurtling down the road at breakneck speed was a County Sheriff cruiser with lights blaring and siren screaming. They heard it that far off. What was remarkable about the whole affair is that they took the time to get in sync with each other before bellowing their disapproval of the approaching vehicle.

Now a days, all of our dogs sing in eight part harmony when a siren is detected off in the distance. We call them the "Rosswood Choir" and the two males sing tenor (a slightly higher tone to their baying). It's quite a thing to behold. Tales from the Bark Side could easily be called Tales From the Bay Side. We do have a few crooners here.

CHAPTER 32

OUT OF SIGHT, OUT OF MIND

It's time to tell a tale about two of my dogs who prove dogs can reason. Lara Mee, the matriarch of our kennels resides in the garage most of the winter. She's earned that right and she covets the whelping kennel as her birth right. We had a female named Roxie that also resided in the garage in a transporting kennel at night and then went out to an outside kennel shortly after getting up in the morning... spoiled huh? She is currently being spoiled by a loving family in a home in North Dakota.

I give our dogs nutritious bone like biscuits as treats and for training as well. Canines all over the world are famous for one thing in particular... burying their bone for later consumption. Since we have concrete floors in the garage, it's rather difficult to bury a bone but there are other things a well motivated dog can use for such purposes. For instance, a bag of potting soil left unattended in a corner or in this instance, the wood pile we have for our free standing stove in the living room. It's a staging area for the wood to dry out a bit.

I witnessed something that confirms, in my mind, that dogs can reason and also can be deceptive as well. I came into the garage one morning to let both "girls" out to do their business outside. I opened Lara Mee's kennel first and she headed directly to the water pail for a cool drink of H2O. I then went over to Roxie's kennel, let her out, but she didn't go for the water as she normally does... she headed for the wood pile. She must have heard Lara Mee hiding that bone sometime the previous evening. Her direct line of sight of the wood pile was obstructed by our car which occupies the same garage.

While Lara Mee was slurping away with unbridled abandon, Roxie was pawing at some hidden treasure in the other corner, stopping every now and then to see where her rival was. Viola! She found a biscuit and then headed back to her kennel.

By now Lara Mee knew something was amiss because Roxie wasn't by her side drinking away like she always does. She cocked her head to one side, stretched her neck to sneak a peek at the other dog, and then realized that her hidden treasure was being pilfered. What happened next is what this story is all about... reasoning.

Roxie was faced with a dilemma. Lara Mee was coming around the car looking for her biscuit. Roxie dropped the biscuit on the floor of her kennel and then promptly sat on the evidence. She had the look of a not so innocent child who has just been caught with her hand in the proverbial cookie jar. Lara Mee stood there in wonder, trying to figure out where the purloined biscuit went.

She resigned herself to going outside and the younger dog sat down, pulled the bone shaped biscuit out, and enjoyed her treat with a look on her face only a photo could capture. Another Kodak moment I missed. You can't carry a camera around all day but you'd sure like to capture those episodes as they happen. If you don't, you're relegated to writing about them and we all know that a picture is... you know the rest of that sentence.

CHAPTER 33

THE BIG CHILL

It is said that there are no extraordinary people in this world, just normal people forced to do extraordinary things. I believe the same can be said of our animal friends.

It was the first snow fall of the winter in late November, 2005. The temperature had dipped to freezing and things were looking like an ice palace around the property. The pond that lies at the bottom of a hill one hundred yards north of the house was frozen over (and to our chagrin; not entirely). The sun was sinking slowly into the west and the last remnants of the day were waning.

We have kennels behind the house in which we keep most of our German Shepherds. I clean the kennels after the dogs are fed and they are allowed (under supervision) to run free and exercise themselves by chasing each other all over the yard. They come over to me when I'm removing the fecal deposits from each separate kennel and let me know they are around... kind of like letting "dad" know where they are. They are very social animals.

I was just finishing Roxie's kennel and ready for

her to hop back in so I could lock it up. She came running up to me with eyes ablaze and a posture I thought odd at the time. I said, "Come on Roxie, in you go" and she turned away from me and started to run down the hill. She stopped and came closer this time and turned away once more. She didn't bark but I thought something was awry. Then it occurred to me that one other dog was missing, Mandee.

Mandee was evaluated as a potential prize show dog when she was younger... she was only eight months old at the time and Roxie was seven months old. They were for all intents and purposes, still pups. To do what Roxie did that night was extraordinary... to say the least.

I followed Roxie down the hill and into the dark hush of the night where the pond barely reflected any semblance of daylight. There with her neck craning out of the ice was Mandee. She had ran across the ice in fearless frolic and inadvertently found the one place where the ice was the thinnest. My heart was in my throat. She looked up at me with "help me eyes" and a whimper that would melt the coldest heart. What to do!

To make matters worse, I was taking a medication that slowed my heart rate down considerably and I easily ran out of breath. I tried to go in after her wearing only rubber boots. They weren't tall enough to keep the icy water out. The sludge and muck of the shallow shoreline water sucked my footsteps down like a black hole devours stars. I was getting stuck myself.

I knew I had to go for help. Cindy was up in the house busy with her school work at the time and I had to make it up the hill to her as fast as I could. I puffed and panted my way back up the hill and Roxie ran along side of me for a bit, and then turned back toward her fallen kennel mate; to remain with her to give her moral support I believe.

Finally I reached the house after what seemed like an eternity. I conveyed our dilemma to my wife. I found some rope and Cindy threw on some boots and we both jumped into the Dodge pick up and down the hill we went.

I turned the high beams on and there racing back and forth was Roxie waiting impatiently for us. The barely frozen water seemed colder than the bottom side of glacier yet it was able to be broken with each frantic step my wife took. We labored for what seemed like hours and finally Cindy reached her. She threw the rope around Mandee's neck and attached it to her collar and the poor puppy strained even harder to free herself from her frozen confines.

I waded in as far as I could because my wife had Mandee by her collar... but Cindy's boots were filled with ice water and she could hardly move herself. I encouraged Mandee to fight through the water and reach the shore under her own power. I had to know if there was any feeling still left in her limbs. She shook and shivered her way out of the water and Cindy and I staggered back to the truck with Mandee clinging to my out stretched arms.

Barking and voicing her approval was the heroine, Roxie. She ran along side the truck as we headed up the hill with one cold pooch. We wrapped Mandee in blankets and towels, placed her in a portable kennel, turned a portable heater on full blast, and carefully placed it in front of the shivering pup.

We both carried ourselves up the stairs and jumped into a much needed and anticipated shower. The warm water cascading across our half frozen bodies felt like heaven. We couldn't luxuriate in the welcomed warmth of that shower... we had unfinished business below.

We went back downstairs and both realized one thing was missing. I went outside and found Roxie circling the house looking for a clue as to what was going on inside. We brought her in and the two female shepherds spent the rest of the night cuddled together; sharing what warmth there was to be had between them. They looked out at us with adoring eyes that only a rescued dog can show.

Instinct played a limited role in this saga, but the

reasoning powers of an eight month old puppy saved the day for one of our most prized and loved dogs. Mandee to this day doesn't get too close to the pond. Although Roxie has gone on to another home, she will always be a "Rosswood Girl" to us.

CHAPTER 34

STICKY FINGERS (PAWS)

Bubba's Auto Parts store is located in the heart of Otter Tail city (it was named after Gary's son, Josh) and should you visit the establishment, you will be greeted by one or two cats that have complete run of the premises. Adam and Eric are friendly and well behaved cats... or it may seem to the uninitiated patron. Eric is satisfied with his role as the store's resident mouser. He's rather quiet and docile and does his best impression of an area rug, but his counterpart, Adam the not so petty of a thief, keeps everybody on their toes.

Gary told me with a chuckle that Adam is a thief...yep, a thief. A regular customer of Gary's came in one day and in the process of purchasing an item, he left a twenty dollar bill on the counter and in the course of visiting and shopping, the bill disappears. Well, Gary knows the customer very well and believes that he left the money on the counter as he claimed and decides to scour the shop. Lo and behold... the twenty dollar bill was found on the floor in his office... hmmm?

Gary recounts this tale to his wife, Sheila, later that day. Sometimes wives don't always believe their husband's stories whether it's about counting cash or pilfering felines. Sheila had a little trouble with the concept of a cat ripping off the customer's cash.

A day or so goes by and she goes to the store to help with the accounting. Bills of assorted denominations were stacked neatly on the desk in Gary's office and for some reason both Gary and Sheila were standing at the counter when Adam saunters out of the office with a $100 bill neatly folded in his mouth. The two of them stood there in stunned silence. Gary is vindicated by his wife, Adam is caught red handed, and a legend is born.

Who says crime doesn't pay? How did Adam know that the hundred dollar bill was worth more... better yet, where was he going with the money? Gary told me that some people just stop by his shop to visit and play with the kitties. I'd be very careful if I were them... Adam may take to picking pockets.

Ella Grunewald of Fergus Falls sent me a tale about a stray cat that just happened to have an appetite for roasts and pies. Let's see what she has to say.

I grew up on a farm. We always had a dog and cats, but they were never allowed inside the house. Later in life, we had a stray cat come and it was a nuisance as it would have a way of sneaking inside our entry without us seeing it come in.

This entry wasn't heated so during the cold months. I was used to cooling hot leftovers before putting it in the refrigerator later on by sitting it on the cabinet located in our entry way.

One day I had set a casserole of roast on that cabinet to cool. Later, I went to retrieve it and soon discovered the cat had been indoors again. The casserole was found to be broken lying on the floor and its contents, the roast, was a total loss.

Later on I baked a pie and decided to set it on top of the cabinet, approximately six feet high. When I went to take the pie down, I discovered the cat had also been there for there was only a little crust left.

I would always catch the cat and toss it outside. I think my two youngsters enjoyed seeing what the cat would do next and how I would react to it.

When spring came, we always removed the storm door and replace it with a screen door. This door was light weight and we saw the cat open it by the clever use of its paws. I told my husband to outsmart the cat by putting the hinges on the opposite side. We, the family, had a hard time getting used to this but the cat had no problem.

After some time, the cat disappeared and that was a relief. One day my husband and son were in town and my son saw this cat on the sidewalk. He took it back home and proudly came to show me and said, "Guess who is back for dinner?"

This was way back in time during the early "Space Program" years and my daughter said, "This cat has spent a lot of time in space!" She was referring to my tossing the cat out. Eventually, the cat moved on and it was peaceful again.

CHAPTER 35

BUDDIES

We have two tales here that, upon first glance, have nothing to do with each other. See if you can see the common thread that runs through both of them. My first story was submitted by a friend of mine, Trish (Pat) Herder of Ottertail. You can tell how much her pets (thought of as children) mean to her through her stories.

Lex and Little One were nine month old cats (they were more like kittens at that age) that did not get along at all. Spats over food bowls and territoriality issues were a continuous agenda for the Herder household. Suffice it to say, "They were not buds!"

Their home was on the second story of an apartment building and they would jump from the balcony to a window air conditioning unit and then light safely on the ground below. It was a route both of the cats used to perform their daily bodily functions.

One day Little One took the circuitous trip to the yard below only to be greeted by the next door neighbor's boyfriend's Pitt Bull...who at the time saw the frightened feline as a tasty chew toy. The Pitt Bull was snarling and approaching the arched back

166

kitty with evil on his mind. Up on the second story, Lex was watching this all play out and something inside of him... the bigger cat gene called out to him. A primal urge of magnificent proportion demanded immediate action.

Lex didn't take the route Little One chose. He literally flew off the balcony with all four legs extended (if it wasn't such a serious moment, you would have thought he was doing his best "Rocky the flying Squirrel" imitation) and landed on the ground on all four feet directly in front of the raging Pitt Bull. The dog changed his demeanor immediately and started to back away from Little One. What happened next is remarkable. Lex backed the larger animal into a corner and eventually out of the yard.

From what Pat tells me, the two cats were the best of friends after that... well, kind of like buddies. The "I can argue, fuss, and fight with my own family but don't you dare say something bad about them" point of view comes to mind. Thanks Pat, for "The Tale of Two Kitties."

Leslie Aschnewitz of Dent, Minnesota called me up one night and recounted a time when he had a Yellow Lab name Brownie that would go duck hunting with him on Saturdays. The two them would go to a nearby mud lake not far from Leslie's house. Brownie was a wonderful retriever and would faithfully jump in the water after the downed fowl that his master had just shot. Good dog, that Brownie.

What was unusual about this fine Yellow Lab is that when her master couldn't make his Saturday hunting trip, unbeknownst to Leslie, Brownie would set off by herself to go patrol a nearby lake. As if that wasn't enough, she'd bring home a trophy for her master almost every time... yes, she'd come marching into the yard with a duck of some sort in her mouth and proudly present it to her puzzled master. Leslie thought at the time it was a wounded duck his retriever had found...but every time the dog went out?

The days, months, and years passed and Brownie would either go with Leslie or go by herself...it was a normal occurrence for the Aschnewitz family but still a mystery of where Brownie was getting her infamous fowl.

Twenty five years later, Leslie was back at one of his favorite hunting spots he frequented in the old "Brownie" days and he encountered several hunters that had been returning there to hunt for years upon years. As in normal conversation about hunting, the subject of retrievers came up. This one man was telling a tale about this Yellow Lab that would come over to where they had their duck blind and retrieve ducks from the lake for the group. In appreciation for her capable assistance in bringing back the fine feathered fowl; they'd reward her with a duck to take home.

Leslie, after hearing this, knew that the dog of which they spoke was his faithful retriever. As he spoke of his long time friend I could hear the love in his voice... the pure admiration for his sweetie, his dog, and his hunting partner. Leslie would almost always have duck for dinner on weekends; whether or not he went hunting with Brownie. It was like Brownie had to deliver on her personal promise of supplying ducks during hunting season.

Now, I pose the question again... what did these two stories have in common? The cats who became buddies after a brush with death and the self appointed "designated retriever" had one important commonality... loyalty. They were bonded to each other with a love and loyalty only a true buddy can give... no matter which specie; no matter what gender.

Instinct plays an important role for retrievers... it's in their DNA to go after a fallen fowl that their master (mistress) has brought down from the autumn skies with one sure shot. But, to go out by yourself to retrieve for a complete (maybe not a complete stranger by this time) stranger and as if acting like a designated retriever on retainer, bring home the goods to her master? That has to be some well reasoned thought processes going on.

Loyalty plays a significant role in animal behavior.

Whether it is directed towards a fellow canine or feline, it doesn't matter. What matters, I believe, is that an unconditional love exists; that overrides any other emotion or feelings... many times over coming abject fear.

CHAPTER 36

THE BACHELOR

The question of whether or not dogs and cats can reason can not be denied... but there are plenty of examples of other species doing some mental processing as well. The animal kingdom operates on another plane of awareness and here is an example that proves the point precisely. Marlo Henneman of Ashby (She also lives on Bluebird Road) sent me this tale. It's about a bachelor bluebird that had his own peculiar problems with the opposite sex.

We live on Bluebird Road...a name I was able to pick because we are the lone dwelling on it. Adjoining landowners who were present before us had established a Bluebird Trail with a series of bluebird houses along the road & we just picked up where they left off. Now we have bluebirds right down in our yard every summer living in the specially designed bluebird houses & bathing in our birdbath.

This story concerns one male bluebird who became captivated by an unusual birdhouse on a big old oak tree just outside my over-the-sink kitchen window. It was an ordinary wood birdhouse with a pitched roof but instead of one entry, it had three although there was only one room inside. Something about this particular house attracted our little home seeker & he was determined to make it his own. Mother Nature provides her creatures with schedules for nesting & the time had come to begin the process. I enjoyed seeing this beautiful brightly colored bird come every day for four or five days and spent at least an hour, sitting on the same spot and flying from time to time in and out of the birdhouse. He would go in one entry hole and come out another after spending a little time inside... choosing different routes each time.

I looked out one day to see if he'd arrived & saw he had a companion. He was accompanied by a pretty little female bluebird. As I watched the pair of them I imagined that he was regaling her with the desirability of moving into a bluebird house that would be the envy of all the other birds. She sat near him on the wire & appeared to listen. I wondered how she would respond. It didn't take long to find out. The lady flew in one door, stayed just a moment and flew out again... right into the wild blue yonder. She never took a second look and she didn't even stop to say goodbye.

This same scenario took place on three different days over a period of a week. There was no way of telling if these females were always the same bird or if he was playing the field but the result was always the same. No deal. After two summers we moved the house just in case it was the location that determined the refusals but after it was moved another species took up residence.

A bluebird family set up housekeeping in a nearby regular ordinary bluebird house but we have no way of knowing if it was our little friend. We can only hope that he did find a home, a mate and that he could forget about his lonely vigil in front of the house that he couldn't have.

Here at Rosswood, we sit and watch our birds in action. I can't say I have seen a bluebird obsessed with a bird house like Marlo Henneman has at her place, but there is plenty of cunning and guile on display to make one believe that they are using their smarts and not their instincts. Still, when it is time to fly south, I don't see them consulting a Rand McNally. A lot of what birds do is strictly instinct. I believe our blue friend may be an exception or was he really thinking of ways to impress a female. Aren't bachelors all alike? Food for thought (in this case bird food).

CHAPTER 37

OOPS!

Perhaps you remember the "Donovan" song from the sixties, 'Mellow Yellow'... and the lyrics, 'I'm just mad about Saffron'? Saffron was a unique looking dog that was a cross between a German Shepherd and a Rhodesian Ridgeback. Her body was that yellowish saffron brown with a red rippled ridge down the middle of her back. If you took both of her ears in your hands and lifted them up, you'd see the shepherd in her, but they hung down upon the side of her face like a blood hound. When she alerted both ears came up and a prominent ridge protruded from her back about four inches high. She was a sight to see.

It was a joy to watch her hunt in tall grass because she'd launch herself off the ground with all four feet in the air at the same time. She'd spring herself across a field hoping to catch a glimpse of whatever she was tracking at the time. I'm told that the lion hunting dogs in Africa (from which the breed beckons) "bound" like that because of the tall grass on the Serengeti Plain. They are fearless dogs that will tackle almost anything.

Being on an island means your only means of

transportation is a boat (or a water plane which I didn't have at the time) and where there is a boat; you'll have incidents that bare retelling. Harbor Island is located on the North Channel of Lake Superior and Lake Huron in Ontario eight miles north of Manitoulin Island. It was built by Benson Ford (One of Henry Ford's Nephews) as a retreat for the Great Lakes Cruising Club shortly after World War II.

I had the use of several types of boats at the resort but my favorite was a fifteen foot steel boat with a ten horsepower outboard motor. I could crank it down and troll for Northern Pike or use it for putting around the other side of the island or go for groceries eight miles across the north channel to a town called Kagawong (I know, it sounds like it should be in China somewhere).

Saffron would station herself in the bow of the boat and let the wind whip threw her hair as if she was on a Harley rolling down a back road in Middle America. She loved it! One of the things that Saffron did that had me a bit concerned and that was her fascination with dragonflies. They would hover above her just beyond her reach and tantalize Saffron until she did something irreversible.

It was a sunset that you might find on a travel brochure and the water was like glass... oranges and purples, grays, and pinks melting into postcard perfection. It was stunning. The resort business happened to slow down and I was going to fish a bit. There were trophy sized Northerns in those waters and I aimed to get me one.

We had just turned the corner of the island where the channel runs past at alarming speed and at that confluence was where Saffron met her dragonfly. It dipped and it soared and it flew in circles around her... and it was driving her crazy at the same time. Then it happened. It was like watching a shopping cart roll down an incline headed for a shiny Cadillac; there was nothing I could do and helpless I truly was.

Rhodesian Ridgebacks have that one characteristic I mentioned before... they can spring up into the air with a single leap; all four feet leaving the ground simultaneously. I wasn't going very fast for there were shoals all about the island that you could damage a boat in a heartbeat (even a steel one). Saffron flew at least three feet into the air and snapped her jaws at a dragonfly that was just beyond her reach.

My memory recalls many things that occurred years ago... this one is crystal clear. I think it was the look on her face that emblazoned that snapshot in time upon my mind. She got the dragonfly... half of it was hanging out the side of her mouth. Her big brown eyes were wide open in sudden and instant realization... she was not on the boat any longer. She frantically pawed at the air as I went past her and then went into the drink with a thunderous splash.

Poor baby! She came up sputtering and the dragonfly was still hanging from the corner of her mouth... limp as a freshly boiled string of fettuccini. I had her spit it out and she was reluctant to do so because, in her mind I believe, that dragonfly was paid for dearly.

When we hearken back in time in our minds, it seems everything is in slow motion. I wonder what the look on that Boston Terrier's face conveyed? Terror? Did Owen immediately know he made a colossal mistake? I'm sure Saffron was more surprised than anything. She still stationed herself in the bow of boat but she snarled and growled at the flying menaces as their taunted from beyond her reach. Saffron stayed put... evidently, she learned a lesson which in itself was a great feat for her. I was learning humility... she was learning patience.

CHAPTER 38

OF MICE AND MEN AND BARN CATS

Saffron and her gangly pup, Strider, were not the only pets we had on the island resort. Now it is the time to tell you about the rest of the family... Cheech and Chong (I'm not talking about Cheech Marin and Sammy Chong, either).

Harbor Island sits in the middle of the North Channel of Lake Superior and Lake Huron in the Great lakes. It measures thirty acres and the only way on the island is by boat or seaplane... or an eight mile swim from Manitoulin Island. Can we say isolated?

I met a man who ran the local bakery in Wawa, Ontario, Canada and he convinced me to manage a resort for him the next summer. It sounded like fun to me. I was twenty seven and quite full of myself at the time and figured I could do just about anything. Boy, did I have a lot to learn!

We had to wait until mid June for the ice to melt on the North Channel to be able to access the resort. The water was colder than Saddam Hussein's heart. The first night that we (a lady named Joan, one named Joanne, and a French Canadian named Edgar) spent on the island by ourselves, there was a plethora of visitors.

One of the ladies had mice caught in her hair and her screaming woke us all with a start. It took several minutes to get the vermin out of her hair. She was deliriously overcome with terror. It seems that the mice and rat population fared quite well over the winter and they were everywhere once the lanterns went out. It was decided then and there that we would go to the main island in the morning (actually the crack of dawn... no one slept after that) and procure a couple barn cats to quell the infestation.

The eight mile journey across the channel seemed to take forever and when we reached the shore, we found out from the local grocery clerk where we might find a few cats. With the help of a borrowed car, off we went looking for the farm that might have the solution to our mice problem.

The farmer wasn't at home at the time we arrived but his wife told us to stay and served us freshly baked biscuits with butter and strawberry jam. The day was looking up indeed. Farmer Brown (I can't remember his real name) finally arrived and took us out to the large red barn that he said housed two especially good mousers. He claimed he never fed these cats... what they ate is what they caught themselves. That sounded good to us.

The next chore we had to perform was to catch

them. He stood back and watched the follies that followed. It was abundantly apparent that these two cats didn't want to be caught. It took all five of us forty five minutes to put those two cats into two burlap sacks. I think all four of us suffered scratches of some sort... the farmer remained unscathed. He smiled and wished us luck. We needed it.

We took advantage of the opportunity to buy groceries while we were on Manitoulin Island... meanwhile the two sacked cats grew increasingly hostile within their burlap prisons. The boat we used to navigate the channel was a twenty one foot Cedar Strip speed boat with a fifty horsepower outboard motor. As light as the boat was, it could fly across the water at a pretty good clip.

There was a storage compartment in the bow of the boat and it had two doors that kept our cargo from spilling out. A gig saw pattern adorned these doors and they bore the rope and anchor design seen on many aquatic craft. There was a brass latch (hasp) that held the two doors together and it was snuggly fastened.

The North Channel is famous for its four foot chops. The water is deep enough for freighters to navigate and when the wind is blowing as hard as it can blow, the waters are treacherous. We were being constantly pounded as we powered our way back to Harbor Island. Eight miles doesn't sound like much but on water that is white capped and constantly slapping at the bow of your boat, it can feel like an eternity... especially if you are a barn cat stowed away in a burlap sack in the bow of the boat.

At first I didn't see the paw in the rope and anchor cutout. One of the crew observed it first. As the bow of the Cedar Strip crashed into the oncoming four foot waves, one of the cats had freed themselves from their sack and was attempting to get out by unlatching the hasp. There was this tiny paw reaching through the cutout trying frantically to flip the latch up. At first, I thought it was quite humorous. Then it struck me; I had to open the doors and attempt to put the cat back in its burlap confines.

This went on for a while so when it did get the doors open, Edgar's size twelve boot was placed strategically; keeping the doors from opening and letting loose the demons from Pandora's box. We reached the dock with Edgar still positioned at the bow of the boat while the two paws of an extremely frightened cat dug away at the latch. We still hadn't solved the dilemma. How were we going to corral the cat and transport it to the cabin without being bitten, scratched, or maimed by a very angry feline? What to do?

The ladies took the groceries to the cabin and left the decision making process to me since I was the manager (and the captain always goes down with the ship they say). Edgar wasn't too pleased with his position and his leg was beginning to cramp up on him also. I slid up next to Edgar and he removed his foot while I placed mine next to where his had been. We both sat facing each other... both of us with goofy grins on our faces. I said, "One, Two, Three, Go!" We both reached down and pulled the doors open and out sprung one of the cats.

It bounced off my chest as I swiped at it and missed. Edgar almost got the tail as he unsuccessfully flailed away as it zoomed pass him. I think he was relieved that he didn't catch it by the tail. The cat bounded once more off the seats of the boat and sprinted down the dock towards the main building. It disappeared in an instant. Edgar looked at me with this stupid look on his face and with his heavy French Canadian accent proclaims, "Boss, I tink da cat is outta da bag!" We both broke up laughing.

The other sack was undulating back and forth and this tremendous yowl was coming from inside. I picked up the sack and a long set of claws were protruding from it. I very carefully brought the contents to the cabin, alerted the ladies of what I was about to do and literally let the cat out of the bag. It made for a bedroom, hid under a bed, and caterwauled for about an hour.

We didn't sleep any better that night because the cabin was filled with the sound of scurrying feet and thumps, thuds, and other noises we didn't really want to identify. We awoke that morning and found a lot of carcasses and a multitude of mice and rat tails. We cleaned them up immediately... by order of the ladies. The barn cat that we kept inside we called Cheech... the outside cat was Chong. Both cats had swollen bellies for what seemed like weeks.

They eventually came to us with a look of satisfaction on their faces and we fed them table scraps and freshly caught fish. They loved their island resort... but that ride over had been murder.

CHAPTER 40

MOTHER GOOSE AND RUEBEN

Whenever I sit down at the computer to write, one thing is bound to happen. If I'm alone, I'm not for long. Usually (if she's down in the garage below) Lara Mee will make the climb up the steep stairs that lead to this large room. This is no easy task for a hundred and twenty pound female shepherd. She has an insatiable need to be by my side or in the immediate area.

I think she likes me sitting in one place so that she can receive the optimum amount of attention. It's become a combination war of wills and hand to paw combat; with a little obsessive compulsive petting on her part thrown in for good measure. With that said, we have a really good relationship and there is a tale that bears re-telling and it's about relationships; those between man (or woman) and beast or those between different species of animals themselves.

This tale has to be one of the most incredible things I've seen in my entire life so far; bar none. My first story about Lady was about a White Collie who saved a barn from burning down one night. She was such a great dog that I saved (what I think) the best "Lady" story until now for a reason...it's just that incredible.

How many of you have had a female dog run off (or break out) when they were in "heat"? It can be a major problem if they mate with some other dog that you have no idea of their lineage or ancestry. Those with pure bred dogs especially are concerned. Also, when you have no idea who the father is, you really don't have a clue what the pups will look like or exactly what breed they are.

Let me say this right here: I think mutts, crossbreeds, mixed breeds, and Heinz fifty seven breeds can be and have been the most even tempered, smartest, and best family dogs ever. They just love you... no pedigree can match that, but then again, we are talking relationships and whatever the breed of the dog or cat (for that matter) it all depends on how they are treated and how they respond to that treatment. I breed German Shepherds because I love that breed and want to improve on the breed by being very selective in my breeding regimen... but I digress. Back to Lady.

My father was a good man. Lady was in heat and she was gone and it was a typical Washington summer day... raining. He searched for her well into the night and finally gave up looking after hours of weary wet work. She was gone. The family was in an uproar and he knew how much we loved our barn saving canine. He decided that when (and if) we got her back and since we didn't know who the father (or fathers) was, it'd be better if we had her spayed. There would be no unwanted pups or mixed breeds of who knows what. His decision was final. I kind of wanted her to have pups just to see what she'd have. My vote didn't count.

Three days later, this mangled mess of mud, hair, and weeds came crawling back. My mother being the pragmatist of the group said, "She looked like something the cat dragged in." I thought it would have to be a really big cat. The next day, she was brought to the veterinarian and the operation was performed.

A few days later, we got her back in basically the same shape as when we sent her in... a matted mess. She needed a bath badly. Long haired dogs are such a joy sometimes. In the fifties, dog grooming wasn't as much a priority as the care and well being of large animals. My folks didn't want to spend the extra money to have her shampooed when we could do it ourselves at home.

On the way home, we stopped at the local co-op store because we needed feed for our other critters...and dog shampoo for our wayward woman. Over in the corner of the store was a table with a wooden box on it and a heat lamp dangling over the box. From within came the unmistakable sound of cheeping chicks. At least I thought they were chicks at the time.

They were fuzzy yellow little goslings just as cute as they could be. After much pleading on my part, my mother decided we would take two of them home with us. I was ecstatic. The rain had stopped the day before and it was a bright sunny beautiful day. When we returned home, a large tub was placed in the front yard and Lady was given a much overdo bath very carefully.

We were brushing the newly clean canine when the goslings were brought outside into the sun. They waddled as fast as their little webbed feet would carry them; straight for Lady. She curled up in a half circle and they nuzzled her with their beaks picking out fleas from her fur. She loved it. They loved her. To this day, we all felt that the baby geese must have thought she was "Mommy" because they imprinted with her on that sunny day.

They followed her to the back porch where she had her kennel under the stairs. This was the most unlikely trio you'd ever imagine. She would walk along with these two fowl friends in tow. As they became adult geese, they still followed her around the farm. I still can see her running at a gallop from the barn to the house with two white geese flying on each side of her.

You may already know this, but in case you don't; geese make better watchdogs than dogs do themselves. In fact, the distilleries in Scotland (where they make all that wonderful scotch) have double wire fencing around their perimeter. Inside that double fencing are gaggles of hissing geese that honk incessantly if anyone even comes near the fences. They sound the alarm with a cacophony of blood chilling chaos. Our two geese would have been on the A team of that group of geese.

Lady did her guard duty well and with the help of her two slightly different children, she protected us from whatever danger that we would have encountered. It's all about relationships. Some of the strangest ones are merely born out of love.

I raised two domestic geese on a ten acre farm I was leasing in British Columbia after I returned west from running the island resort near Manitoulin Island in Ontario, Canada. Rueben was a grey gander and Charmer was his lovely white goose. They were prolific poopers and left their presents all over the yard. It was something that you really didn't want to slip on and fall upon.

I had a friend named Eric that had the most beat up looking VW bug that I have ever seen in my entire life. Once upon a time it was a nice shiny black. When Eric took possession of it, the paint was peeling off in strips. It looked like it had vehicular psoriasis.

One day, Eric drove into the yard in that junk heap and Rueben came waddling over to it with his head bowed and his hiss on full volume. He started to peck at the blistering paint on the driver's side door and was running his head back and forth like an old Remington manual typewriter (only there was no "ding" when he reached the end of his row).

Eric was too scared to get out of his dilapidated VW. He screamed at me from his captive seat, "Keith, call off your guard goose, will ya?" I laughed for a long time. He was getting more anxious and yelled once again, "I'm serious; your goose is attacking my car and me. I won't have any paint left when he is done!" I thought that was actually a good thing. I eventually gave in and shooed Rueben away from my friend and his freshly detailed bug. It's all about relationships.

CHAPTER 42

THE BIRDMAN OF MENLO PARK

I believe that some people come into your life for a reason. They touch your heart in many ways and leave an indelible mark upon your soul. Tony Gouveia was one of those kinds of people for me. The funny thing about his legacy with the birds is... I never knew about them until he was late into a hospital stay from which he would never leave.

Tony was from a very large and prominent family in the Santa Clara Valley and was an owner of a taxi company and thusly associated with being a "city boy". He was this portly little guy that was balding and sort of reminded you of a civilized "Louie DePalma" from the television series, Taxi.

Tony was a veteran of the Korean War and didn't wear the cloak of combat fatigue publicly but I suspect he had his personal demons like all combat soldiers. He smoked and even at the end of his life, wasn't about to quit. He lived life mostly on his terms and was defiant to the smoking Nazis to the end. He was considerate to his friends so he went out side to smoke long before it was mandated by law.

I used to visit him at the Menlo Park Veteran's

Hospital and he would wheel himself down a long corridor to the front doors and he would have his cigarette break outside. He did this everyday for a few years and so when I came to visit him one particular day, I was surprised to see him with a bag full of unsalted peanuts resting inconspicuously on his lap.

I asked him, "when did you start eating peanuts"? (Tony had false teeth and I thought the nuts would be hard to eat.) He smiled this ignominious smile of his and said, "They're not for me". I looked over my glasses at him, as he sat in his wheelchair puffing away on a Marlboro, and gave him my patented raised eyebrow look.

We had been friends a long time and I knew I was being set up for something short of extraordinary. I imagined he had a squirrel or a chipmunk that would be the recipient of his generosity and they would come willing to receive his gift.

He finished his smoke and wheeled himself closer to the sidewalk and turned around to face me. He pulled a peanut out of the bag and held it above his head with his right hand extended; the peanut firmly grasped between his thumb and forefinger. At first, I thought he was making the "OK" sign but all of a sudden, out of the clear blue sky, dove a flash of blue and a flap of white feathers and then it was gone.

He smiled from ear to ear. "These are my birds" he proudly announced to me and several other people milling around behind me. Some of them must have seen this trick before because they obviously weren't as impressed as I. Once again he held out his hand again and this time I was looking for it and there, coming off the ledge above the main entrance, was a Blue Jay flapping his way towards Tony and the properly presented peanut.

I've seen eagles fishing and their outstretched talons gripping a flopping fish in their grasp. I've seen hummers turn sideway to sip a bit of nectar from a feeder... but I never seen a Blue Jay pick a peanut from someone's hand with its beak before. Stan Tekiela (a well know ornithologist) describes the common specie as "being the alarm of the forest" and signals a loud shriek when an intruder approaches.

That was a far cry (no pun intended) from deep forests I know but being tamed to fetch elephant food is a remarkable achievement. I asked Tony if he was the trainer of these birds or did he inherit the trick from a former resident? He answered in his variation of yes by whistling through his teeth at the same time saying si'. He really never did answer my question but in my mind he was THE trainer.

I brought my wife to be up from San Jose to visit Tony one day and I hadn't told her of his skullduggery with the birds. When we escorted him outside and he had his obligatory cigarette, he performed his little feat for her. She was amazed. Then the ailing man handed me a peanut and told me to hold it up for them. I did as I was told and was delighted when I accomplished the same result as my friend.

I handed one to Cindy and, being the trusting person I had come to love and adore, she held it above her... proud and brave. And viola! It snatched the peanut from her hand with the deftness of a New Orleans pickpocket. She giggled in response. I was beginning to wonder if Tony hadn't come along and perpetuated a long lived ritual but he claimed he trained them. I chose to believe a dying man.

A city boy who trained a wild jay to pick peanuts from his hand? What was the world coming to? From the reaction of the fowl, who is known for its adversarial disposition, that loved to swoop down and grab a goodie from a terminally ill patient, I'd say the world is doing just fine. Tony left a legacy that still exists today. If you should wander into the San Francisco Bay area, be sure to visit Menlo Park and the peanut grabbing Blue Jays at the Veteran's Hospital.

Once again, it's all about relationships. The ones between man and beast or fowl seem to be the ones that have meaning beyond our perception. We love them and they give back without expectation and unconditionally. What more could we ask for?

I think back at all the pets I have had and their idiosyncrasies, and I truly smile. You should too. For tales from the bark side of life is about the life we live with our four legged and two legged friends. I will leave you with this little poem. Until Next Time.

Keith Alan Ross

IN MEMORY OF

Two sunset silhouettes facing west
The master and his dog
Each one believing
The other one to be the best

A purr-fect furry friend
Ten tons of toes
One foot at a time
Across a moonlit bed

Paw prints in the snow
And winter wails against
A weathered window pane
And a chickadee feeds in solace

A nocturnal solo sojourn
Cries of lovely life
A curled lady in slumber
Puppy breath for breakfast

Waiting canine cuties
Beautiful bus stop buddies
Barnyard bellows from beyond the fence
Once upon a farm

My ebony shepherd smiling
Dawn in the distance shining
Clear skies awaiting
Unsung sacrifices of a friend

Days of sad eyed Bassets
And prancing purple Poodles
Silly Saint Bernards drooling
Yellow Labs adoring infant smiles

Like movies
In my mind
Like magic
Made in kind

Faces of the friends
Loyal loving to the end
My heart still warms aglow
Of the creatures I've come to know

They leave us better than they found us...just
by their coming into our lives.

TO REORDER "TALES FROM THE BARK SIDE"
Mail this form with your check or money order to:

KEITH ALAN ROSS
38589 CTY HWY 1 • RICHVILLE, MN 56567

Name: _____

Mailing Address: _____

City: _____ State:_____ Zip Code:_____

TALES FROM THE BARK SIDE .... **$16.99 each**

Please send me _____ books
Add $3.95 for shipping and handling.
Add $2.00 for each additional book ordered,

- -

TO REORDER "TALES FROM THE BARK SIDE"
Mail this form with your check or money order to:

KEITH ALAN ROSS
38589 CTY HWY 1 • RICHVILLE, MN 56567

Name: _____

Mailing Address: _____

City: _____ State:_____ Zip Code:_____

TALES FROM THE BARK SIDE .... **$16.99 each**

Please send me _____ books
Add $3.95 for shipping and handling.
Add $2.00 for each additional book ordered,